TELLING
TIME

A HARVEST ORIGINAL

HARCOURT BRACE & COMPANY

New York   San Diego   London

NANCY WILLARD

TELLING
TIME

· · · · ·

Angels, Ancestors,
and Stories

Acknowledgment

I am indebted to the community of writers at the Bread Loaf Writers'
Conference, where many of the essays in this volume were first presented as "craft lectures."

Copyright © 1993, 1991, 1982 by Nancy Willard

Permissions follow page 267

Library of Congress Cataloging-in-Publication Data
Willard, Nancy.
Telling time / Nancy Willard.—1st ed.
p.   cm.
I. Title.
PS3573.I444T4   1993
814'.54—dc20   93-16390

Designed by Lisa Peters
Printed in the United States of America
First edition
A B C D E

For Sue and Paul Wehmeier

TABLE OF CONTENTS

Time is but the stream I go a-fishing in. I drink at it; but while I drink I see the sandy bottom and detect how shallow it is. Its thin current slides away, but eternity remains. I would drink deeper; fish in the sky, whose bottom is pebbly with stars.

Henry David Thoreau
Walden

TELLING
TIME

HOW POETRY CAME INTO THE
WORLD AND WHY GOD
DOESN'T WRITE IT

• • • • • • • • •

$\int$everal months ago I walked into a bookshop determined not to buy a book and saw, among the remainders, a small volume called *The Lost Books of Eden*. It beckoned to me like the serpent poised at the Tree of Knowledge. I considered the price. I considered my purse. I said to myself, Opening that book could be dangerous to my economy, and I went out. Instead of leaving the scene of temptation, I walked around the block. When the bookshop came into view, I remembered the parable: The kingdom of heaven is like unto a man seeking goodly pearls who, when he had found one pearl of great price, went and sold all that he had and bought it. Also, wisdom is better than rubies, knowledge is better than gold, and so on. Nothing makes us more vulnerable to temptation than ignorance. I had to know what was in that book.

Alas! When I looked for the book, it was gone. The clerk was sorry. *The Lost Books of Eden* had just been sold. Since that time I have speculated on what it might have contained. I have nearly reconstructed the lost books of Eden in my head. My reconstruction goes light on doctrine and heavy on losses.

I see myself as an insurance salesman. Adam and Eve have found their way to my office. They draw up two vinyl-covered chairs and tell me their tragedy. They have lost everything through an act of God.

"Can you be more specific?" I say, shuffling through my papers for the right forms. "Exactly what did you lose?"

"Eternal life," says Adam.

"The roses I'd just planted in the western bower," says Eve.

"My free time," says Adam.

"My animals," says Eve. "Even the hummingbirds were eating out of my hand."

"Poetry," says Adam.

"Poetry," says Eve.

"Poetry?" I exclaim. "Well, that's the first thing you've mentioned that *can* be replaced. There's plenty of poetry outside of Eden."

"But it's not the same here as it was there," says Adam. "Poetry was invented in Eden. There was a well in the garden. Anytime you put your ear to it, you heard a poem. Anytime you drank from it, you spoke poems. Poetry was so easy. No waiting, no revising, no dry spells."

"Where does the Bible tell how God invented poetry?" I ask.

"God didn't invent it," says Adam. "I did."

"I did too," says Eve. "Remember me?"

"Where does it say so in the Bible?" I demand.

"In the books that were lost," says Adam. "The lost books of Eden. You don't believe me?"

"I don't know what to believe," I answer.

"Look, pretend you're in Eden," says Eve. "God has just spent six days inventing the animals and the birds and the plants, and He's exhausted. He hasn't invented poems; there are some things only humans can make. Unless you want to call the sun and the moon and the birds and the beasts God's poems. Unless you want to call Adam His first reader."

"When God made me in His own image, He made me a creator too," says Adam. "And let me tell you, this creation business interested me a good deal. Especially after God let me name everything. The plants weren't too hard, except there were so many of them. I'd look at a plant and say the first sound that came into my head. And that sound would write itself in letters of gold on the air: *sycamore*, *turnip*, *ginkgo*, *parsley*. Later, in the cool of the evening, God stopped by to see how things were going.

" 'Did you name them all? You didn't forget any of My weeds?'

" 'Not a one,' I told Him.

" 'Nice work, Adam,' said God. 'Now I want you to name the animals.'

"One by one, the animals filed by me and waited to see what I would call them. A low beast with pointed ears and long whiskers came by, softly, softly. I said the first sound that came into my head: 'Cat.'

"And the name wrote itself on the air in letters of gold: *C-A-T*.

" 'That's what you think,' said the cat. 'That's what you call me. But it's not what I call myself.'

" 'What do you call yourself?' I asked.

" 'I am he who counteracts the powers of darkness with my electrical skin and glaring eyes,' announced the cat.

"The cat's name for himself also appeared on the air in letters of gold.

" 'To me you're *cat,*' I tell him. 'Next!'

"Another small beast hopped up. A beast with long ears and a brief tail. And again I said the first sound that came into my head: 'Hare.'

"The name hung in the air for a moment before it floated down to the grass. Nice, short, easy to say.

" 'That's my first name,' said the little beast, 'but not my last.'

" 'What is your last name?'

" 'Which one?' asked the hare. 'There's *jumper* and *racer.* There's *hug-the-ground* and *frisky legs.* There's *long-lugs, grass-biter, dew-hammer, race-the-wind, jig-foot*—'

" 'Wait!' I exclaimed.

" 'There's *creep-along, sitter-still, shake-the-heart, fern-sitter, hedge-squatter*—'[1]

"The names were writing themselves in the air like crazy.

" 'You're *hare* to me,' I said.

"The animals took their names politely, but they also kept their own, and they let me know that those were their real names. At the end of the day, names sparkled in heaps on the grass; the garden was littered with them. I gathered them up and threw them in the well under the Tree of Knowledge. But they didn't sink out of sight. They stuck together, they made new names, they told one another secrets. I could see that creation was no simple matter.

"So one day I said to God: 'Show me how You made some of this stuff. That snake, for example.'

" 'No,' said God. 'Trade secret. I don't give away My trade secrets.'

" 'How about one little secret? A blade of grass, for example. Or that cat sitting in the grass.'

"God considered the cat. He considered it all at once, eternally, from its alpha to its omega.

" 'It's a funny thing,' said God, 'but I don't thrill to it anymore. Except when you do, Adam. What good is creation if nobody enjoys it?'

" 'I enjoy it.'

" 'Tell me about it,' said God.

"I thought hard. What could I tell God about the grass? I sat at the well and poked around for that word to see what happened to it.

" '*Grass!*' I called hopefully.

"To my surprise the word *grass* swam right up like a fish and stayed there, shimmering. I took a big drink from the well. And that evening when God came by to see how things were, I opened my mouth and the well words rolled out. Words about the grass:

A child said *What is the grass?* fetching it to me with full
hands;
How could I answer the child? I do not know what it is
any more than he.

I guess it must be the flag of my disposition, out of hopeful
green stuff woven.

Or I guess it is the handkerchief of the Lord,
A scented gift and remembrancer designedly dropt,
Bearing the owner's name someway in the corner, that we
may see and remark, and say *Whose?*[2]

" 'Nice,' said God. 'That's awfully nice.'

" 'You mean the grass?' I said.

" 'No, the questions. They make Me forget I know all the answers. Can you make them work on something else?'

"And God went away. The next evening I looked around the garden and spied a tyger lounging under the Tree of Knowledge. I looked into the well. There, lazing on the surface of the water, gleamed my questions about the grass. I stirred them back down, and I leaned close to the water.

" *Tyger,'* I said.

"The word *tyger* swam right up, and I took a drink from the well. Later that evening God came by to see how I was doing.

" 'I've got some questions for you, God. Questions about the tyger:

" 'Let's hear them,' said God.

"So I opened my mouth and the well words rolled out. Words about the tyger:

Tyger Tyger, burning bright,
In the forests of the night;
What immortal hand or eye,
Could frame thy fearful symmetry?

In what distant deeps or skies,
Burnt the fire of thine eyes?
On what wings dare he aspire?
What the hand dare seize the fire?

And what shoulder, & what art,
Could twist the sinews of thy heart?

And when thy heart began to beat,
What dread hand? & what dread feet?

What the hammer? what the chain,
In what furnace was thy brain?
What the anvil? what dread grasp,
Dare its deadly terrors clasp?

When the stars threw down their spears
And water'd heaven with their tears:
Did he smile his work to see?
Did he who made the Lamb make thee?

Tyger Tyger burning bright,
In the forests of the night:
What immortal hand or eye,
Dare frame thy fearful symmetry?[3]

" 'I like it,' said God.

"The tyger liked it too. Said the questions made him seem mysterious and important. For a while everything in the garden wanted me to say questions about it. I made questions about the lion and the rose and the wren and the snake and the lamb. I made questions for all of them. It was 'Little lamb who made thee' and 'Little rose who made thee,' and all the creatures in the garden were happy. And every time I said my questions to God, He nodded.

" 'Nice,' He'd say.

"But I could see that God was getting bored. After all, didn't He make everything? Didn't He know it all from the beginning? So I decided to try something new. I'd let God ask the questions. I'd think of something and give Him a couple of clues, and I'd wrap it in images like a gift in a box. And when God guessed what I was thinking of, the box would open.

"For my first gift, I'd start with the well itself.

"The next evening when God came by to see how I was doing, I said:

> As round as an apple,
> As deep as a cup,
> And all God's horses
> Cannot pull it up.[4]

" 'What are you talking about?' said God.

" 'This well,' I said.

" 'Say it again,' said God.

"I said it again.

" 'Nice,' said God. And He looked all pleased. 'The way you made me see it. The way you made it part apple and part cup. The way you made it important. What do you call this thing?'

"I said the first name that came into my head: 'Riddle.'

"For days I went around creation riddling this and riddling that: leaves, flowers, birds, a stone, an egg. I even riddled an egg:

> In marble walls as white as milk,
> Lined with a skin as soft as silk,
> Within a fountain crystal-clear
> A golden apple doth appear.
> No doors are there to this stronghold,
> Yet thieves break in and steal the gold.[5]

"I could see the hen was pleased, but God was getting a trifle bored. Enough riddles already, I thought. I'll try something else. God liked the way I made the well part apple and part cup, and He liked the way I made the egg part marble and silk, part gold and milk, and part crystal. What was the point of making Him say, 'It's an egg' or 'It's a well'? I could just give Him the part He liked: the part where I linked the egg and the well with other things.

"I murmured 'Egg' over the well, and up swam the word. There in the depths of the well twinkled my questions about the tyger and the lamb and the lion and the rose and the snake, and they were tangled up with my riddles about the well and the egg and the stone and the leaves and the birds; you could hardly tell where one started and the other left off. The word *egg* had got so mixed up with other words that I hardly recognized it. It looked as if a dream had rocked it for seven nights running.

"Nevertheless, I took a long, cool drink.

"That evening when God found me in the garden, I said, 'You remember the riddle about the egg.'

" 'Which one?' asked God. 'Weren't there several?'

" 'The one where it turned into marble walls as white as milk.'

" 'Oh yes,' said God. 'That was nice.'

" 'Well, I've got another egg for you. But you don't have to find it. You just have to believe it.'

" 'I'm listening,' said God.

"So I opened my mouth and the well words rolled out:

> In this kingdom
> the sun never sets;
> under the pale oval
> of the sky

there seems no way in
or out,
and though there is a sea here
there is no tide.

For the egg itself
is a moon
glowing faintly
in the galaxy of the barn,
safe but for the spoon's
ominous thunder,
the first delicate crack
of lightning.[6]

" 'You just told me the egg is a moon, and I believed you,' said God, 'I who made the egg and who made the moon. It's a lie. It's like the lies angels tell.'

" 'What other lies are there?' I asked.

" 'Never mind,' said God. 'What do you call it?'

"I said the first name that came into my head: 'Metaphor.'

"And for a long while I was happy. But man cannot live by metaphor alone, or by questions or riddles or even the names of things. And one evening when God stopped by the garden to see how things were going, I said, 'God, I'm depressed. I have this wonderful life in the lovely garden, and I'm depressed.'

"God looked at me for a long time. He looked right through me.

" 'You have a well-stocked mind,' He said. 'But your heart is empty. You need a helpmate.'

" 'Sounds good to me,' I said. 'When will it arrive?'

" 'Making you a helpmate isn't as simple as making a worm or a wren,' said God. 'Adam, I'm going to give you the first general anesthetic.'

"And God caused me to fall into a deep sleep. And when my body was asleep, my spirit climbed out and flew straight to the well and jumped in and came back with all this stuff that the well had made down in the depths: emerald winds, tiger lilies. So now I knew how God made things. God wasn't the only one who could dream. God wasn't the only one who could invent. But He was the only one who could bring it all back.

"In the first fragile moments between waking and sleeping, I thought I had brought something back, perhaps a little corner of the emerald wind speaking in wild green syllables. What I heard on waking was neither bird nor bell nor angel, and it sounded like nothing else in Eden:

> I will give my love an apple without any core,
> I will give my love a house without any door,
> I will give my love a palace wherein he may be
> and he may unlock it without any key.[7]

" 'What's that marvelous sound?' I exclaimed.

" 'That's singing,' said God.

"How can I say what the singing was like? It was not like words rising from the well into my mouth. It was as if the well itself were singing. And hearing that sound for the first time in my life, I was—for the first time in my life—lonely. The singing changed course the way a river does, but it did not end:

> Western wind, when wilt thou blow,
> The small rain down can rain?

Christ, that my love were in my arms
And I in my bed again![8]

"I sprang up, wide awake now. And God took my hand and said, 'Adam, meet Eve. This is your helpmate.'

"She sang, 'Lullay, lullay,' and the birds and beasts tucked their heads under their wings and slept, and she sang, 'Hallelujah!' and everything woke up full of praise. Nobody had ever made those words before. She sang, and the words answered with rhythms of their own. One was like a heartbeat, another like a dance step. As I recognized the different rhythms, I knew that without realizing it I'd been hearing them since the day I was born. I tried to name them so that I could ask for the ones I liked best: *iamb, anapest, trochee.* I'd say to Eve, 'Sing me something in anapests.'

" 'You mean something that sounds like a stone skipping?'

"Sometimes in the middle of her song she'd throw in *lullay lullay* or *hey nonny nonny* or *fiddle dee dee.* And I'd look all over creation for a nonny or a dee, and finally I'd have to ask her, 'What's a fiddle? What's a dee? What's a nonny?' And she'd laugh and say: 'I don't know. It's what the well sings to itself early in the morning. Ask the well.'

"Oh, when she laughed! The stars in their spheres started humming, the morning stars sang together. What were riddles and metaphors to her? She could never remember the names of the iambs and anapests. But let her draw a song around the simplest thing in the world, and I would be filled with joy. And long after I'd forgotten the tune, long after I'd forgotten the words, I could still hear the rhythm of the words, the hum they make when they dance and sing in the well. Who can explain singing? It is a bell weeping and it is a procession of butterflies chanting and it is the tender tread of an elephant walking in its sleep. And whenever I heard Eve singing, I said to myself, 'Though I have the secret names of the angels, if I have not music, I have nothing.' Whenever I made metaphors, I tried to please the ear of God as well as His eye."

Adam stopped talking. It was very quiet in my office. Even the janitor had gone home. I cleared my throat and shuffled my papers and tried to remember why I'd ended up in the insurance business. The reasons eluded me, and I resolved to start looking for another job the next day. Eve blew her nose and wiped her eyes.

"Everyone liked my singing," said Eve, "except the serpent. He'd come by in the morning and listen to me, though. There was one song he always asked for, a song I'd sing when I was off tending the roses in the western bower. I sang it so that Adam would know where to find me:

> It is late last night the dog was speaking of you;
> the snipe was speaking of you in her deep marsh.
> It is you are the lonely bird through the woods;
> and that you may be without a mate until you find me.[9]

"One evening when I sang that song for the serpent, he said: 'It's nice. But something is missing. You sing everything in the same key.'

" 'Key?'

" 'Key,' said the serpent. 'Key is what locks the tune to itself and locks it into your heart. You are singing in the key of C major.'

" 'What other key is there?' I asked.

" 'Why, there are more keys for tunes than roses on that bush. When you've found all the major keys, you haven't even started to discover the noble sorrows of the minor keys. Let me sing your song in one of the minor keys, and you'll see what you're missing.' "

When I go by myself to the Well of Loneliness,
I sit down and I go through my trouble;
when I see the world and do not see my boy,
he that has an amber shade in his hair.

.   .   .   .

My heart is as black as the blackness of the sloe,
or as the black coal that is on the smith's forge;
or as the sole of a shoe left in white halls;
it was you put that darkness over my life.

You have taken the east from me; you have taken the
   west from me;
you have taken what is before me and what is behind me;
you have taken the moon, you have taken the sun from
   me;
and my fear is great that you have taken God from me![10]

"Well, I shivered all over when I heard how the serpent's singing changed things. It was just as if somebody had opened a door in the garden and shown us what we were going to do tomorrow and tomorrow and tomorrow, just as if we could know what only God knew, that our little garden was called out of a sea of darkness, and it could be called back to that darkness. I'd never thought much about the void, though God had told us a little about how it was before the garden came, when darkness covered the face of the deep.

" 'Wise serpent, wily serpent,' I whispered, 'what is the secret of your singing?'

" 'Loss,' hissed the serpent. 'Change. Sorrow. You and Adam live forever in Eden. When he's gone, you don't miss him. You just misplace him.'

" 'And where can I get loss, change, and sorrow?' I begged.

" 'From the Tree of Knowledge,' replied the serpent.

" 'God said if we eat of that tree, we shall surely die,' I said.

"The serpent laughed his flat little breathy laugh.

" 'Did God tell you what death means?' he asked.

" 'He said something about falling asleep forever,' I said. 'To tell you the truth, I didn't pay very much attention.'

" 'Believe me, you won't fall asleep,' the serpent assured me. 'I know. I've eaten from the tree myself. You will be more alive than ever. You will savor every moment. And you will sing the song that makes your bones shiver and your spirit ache with longing.'

" 'But will we fall asleep forever after the song is sung?' I asked.

" 'Eve,' said the serpent, 'you will turn into the greatest gift the tree can offer. Your life will have a beginning and an end. Your life will be a story in the mouths of millions.'

" '*Story,*' I repeated. It wasn't a word I knew. 'Did you find that word in the well?'

" 'I put it there myself,' replied the serpent.

" 'And what does a story look like?' I asked.

" 'Like me,' said the serpent. 'I am the very shape of a story. Story is the thread on which all the other words are strung. It pulls them along, it gives them a purpose in life.'

" 'Is it as good as singing? Is it as good as metaphor?' I asked.

" 'My dear little Eve, story is the river on which metaphor moves and has its being. But it can only live in the fullness of time. That's why God, who lives outside of time, can't tell stories. To Him the alpha and the omega, the once upon a time and the happily ever after, are features on a single face. But you, Eve, shall tell stories. When you have eaten the fruit of the Tree of Knowledge, you shall know the beginning of your life but not the end of it, only that it must end. You'll tell stories whose endings will surprise you, though you are their teller and creator. The Tree of Knowledge will make you wonderfully ignorant.'

" 'And can I sing stories?' I asked.

" 'Your most beautiful stories will be those you sing,' the serpent assured me. 'And when you sing them, broken lives and broken promises will become as lovely and whole as a tear of crystal.'

" 'Sing me a story,' I begged the serpent. 'Sing me a story made of such healing.'

"So the serpent sang:

There lived a wife at Usher's Well,
   And a wealthy wife was she;
She had three stout and stalwart sons,
   And sent them o'er the sea.

They hadna been a week from her,
   A week but barely ane,

When word came to the carlin wife   *carlin:* peasant
  That her three sons were gane.

They hadna been a week from her,
  A week but barely three,
When word came to the carlin wife
  That her sons she'd never see.

'I wish the wind may never cease,
  Nor [fashes] in the flood,   *fashes:* trouble, storms
Till my three sons come hame to me,
  In earthly flesh and blood.'

It fell about the Martinmass,
  When nights are lang and mirk,
The carlin wife's three sons came hame,
  And their hats were o' the birk.   *birk:* birch

It neither grew in syke nor ditch,   *syke:* riverlet
  Nor yet in ony sheugh;   *sheugh:* trench
But at the gates o Paradise,
  That birk grew fair eneugh.

'Blow up the fire, my maidens!
  Bring water from the well!
For a' my house shall feast this night,
  Since my three sons are well.'

And she has made to them a bed,
  She's made it large and wide,

And she's ta'en her mantle her about,
  Sat down at the bed-side.

Up then crew the red, red cock,
  And up and crew the gray;
The eldest to the youngest said,
  ' 'Tis time we were away.'

The cock he hadna craw'd but once,
  And clapp'd his wings at a',
When the youngest to the eldest said,
  'Brother, we must awa'.

'The cock doth craw, the day doth daw,
  The channerin' worm doth chide;   *channerin':* fretting, gnawing
Gin we be mist out o' our place,   *gin:* if
  A sair pain we maun bide.

'Fare ye weel, my mother dear!
  Fareweel to barn and byre!
And fare ye weel, the bonny lass
  That kindles my mother's fire!'[11]

" 'I don't understand the story,' I said, 'but I believe it. What's it about?'

" 'It's about you,' said the serpent. 'The wife is you, the maids are you, the lassie by the fire is you. They're all you. When you have eaten the fruit of the Tree of Knowledge, little Eve, no story will be closed to you.'

" 'Give me knowledge,' I pleaded.

" 'What God calls knowledge I call ignorance,' said the serpent. 'What God calls ignorance, I call story. Help yourself to an apple from the tree that stands in the center of the garden.' "

Silence again fell over the three of us. It would be getting dark outside the office, I thought. I don't have a window; you don't get a window till someone who has one quits or dies.

"So you ate the apple, Madam, and you gave a piece to your husband, and God put you both out of the garden with nothing but your fig leaves," I said, trying to sum up the legalities of the case. "You wish to declare a total loss?"

"No," said Adam, "because we didn't lose everything. When the avenging angel took us to the East Gate, just before he opened it, he turned and said to me, 'You lost eternal life. How could you be so dumb?'

" 'Eternal life never seemed that great,' I said humbly. 'We'd never known anything else. What I really hate to lose is that well.'

"The angel looked surprised.

" 'Why, that's the only thing you haven't lost,' he said. 'God doesn't want the well. What use is it to God? So He's letting you take it with you.'

" 'Where is it?' I asked.

" 'The well is inside you,' replied the angel. 'Much more convenient to carry it that way. Of course, it's not going to be as easy to find as it was in the garden, where you could just lean over and take a drink. Sometimes you'll forget the words you're looking for, or you'll call and the wrong ones will answer. Sometimes they'll be a long time coming. But everything the well gave you it will give you again. Or if not you, your children. Or your great-great-great-great-grandchildren. And since God created you in His image, you have His dream power.

By the grace of dreams we may meet again, blown together by an emerald wind. And I hope you'll remember me with metaphors and make a lovely web of words about me. I hope you'll make some marvelous—what do you call it?'

"I said the first word that came into my head: '*Poetry.*' "

NOTES

[1] Anonymous, "The Names of the Hare," in *The Rattle Bag*, Seamus Heaney and Ted Hughes, eds. (London: Faber and Faber, 1984), 305–6.

[2] Walt Whitman, "Song of Myself," in *Leaves of Grass* (New York: The Heritage Press, 1950), 29.

[3] William Blake, "The Tyger," in *Songs of Innocence and Songs of Experience* (London: Oxford University Press, 1970), Plate 42.

[4] Iona Opie and Peter Opie, eds., *The Oxford Nursery Rhyme Book* (London: Oxford University Press, 1967), 148.

[5] Opie and Opie, 152.

[6] Linda Pastan, "Egg," in *PM/AM* (New York: W. W. Norton Co., 1982), 65.

[7] Anonymous, adapted from "I Will Give My Love an Apple without e'er a Core," in *The Rattle Bag*, 206.

[8] Adapted from "Western Wind . . . ," in *Early English Lyrics*, E. K. Chambers and F. Sidgwick, eds. (New York: October House, Inc., 1967), 69.

[9] Anonymous, "Donal Og," in *The Rattle Bag*, 132–33.

[10] Ibid.

[11] Anonymous, "The Wife of Usher's Well," in *The Viking Book of Folk Ballads of the English Speaking World*, Albert B. Friedman, ed. (New York: The Viking Press, 1956), 35–36.

HIGH TALK IN THE STARLIT WOOD:
ON SPIRITS AND STORIES

• • • • • • • • •

While yet a boy I sought for ghosts, and sped
Through many a listening chamber, cave and ruin,
And starlit wood, with fearful steps pursuing
Hopes of high talk with the departed dead.[1]

—Percy Shelley

It was at Camp Whirlaway in the Irish Hills, not far from Ann Arbor, that I laid claim to my first ghost. I was eleven years old, lying in the top bunk of a room with five other girls. All except myself were in love with horses, at ease with horses. I was the only girl at this camp, which was devoted to horseback riding, who was terrified of horses, and I had chosen this camp because all my girlfriends were going. Nobody told me I would have to canter across fields and gallop down highways. Nobody told me a huge mare would throw me off in a stream and try to roll over on me. Nobody told me that a one-eyed Indian pony would carry me under a low branch and drag me after her, my feet still in the stirrups, the saddle having twisted loose; she had bloated when I saddled her, out of a grudge against me for mounting her on her blind side.

By day I was the girl who was afraid of horses. But at night I was the girl who was not afraid of ghosts. Lying there in the dark, I told my bunkmates about the ghost in my grandmother's house. First I told them about the house. It had belonged to a wealthy doctor whose wife, I assured them, had hung herself in the cellar, and he had sold the house at a loss. The wife's suicide was a lie but the cellar—ah, the terrors of that cellar! Nothing anyone could offer me would have induced me to go down there at night. During the day it was bad enough—walls and walls of cherries put up long ago in jars, aged to a uniform darkness, like food for the dead. Of the shelves of mummified provisions there seemed no end, rising above the sad pale crocks in which Grandmother made sauerkraut. The only friendly spot in the cellar was the round table where my grandfather kept a loaf of bread, a jar of apple butter, and a book on beekeeping. This was his retreat when Grandmother yelled at him. Grandmother was afraid of ghosts. Grandfather was not.

The rest of the house was elegant, I told my listeners, supposing that their grandfathers were all bankers—how else could they afford to keep horses? I told them about the brass carpet rods on the staircase and the chandeliers that hung from the ceiling in every room like crystal wedding cakes. The crystals often came loose, and I would find them everywhere—in drawers, in closets—like tears, as if the house were secretly weeping. The banister in that house was beyond all praise. It was like sliding down a bolt of satin.

I didn't tell them that my grandfather was an osteopath who could not afford to live in this splendid mansion. My grandmother rented out all the rooms except three, plus the kitchen. The first was the

office, where the patients waited under the kindly gaze of Andrew
Still, founder of osteopathy, whose marble bust looked down from a
high bookcase. Beyond lay the treatment room, with its cabinets of
medicines and Grandfather's treatment table, like a flat coffin with a
foot pedal for adjustments. On such a table I imagined Dr. Frankenstein
making his monster, bidding him rise.

The treatment room adjoined my grandmother's bedroom. It was
Grandfather's too, until it grew so crowded that he found it more
convenient to sleep on the fold-out sofa in the office. Grandmother
could not resist a bargain, and she never threw anything away, for
who knew when, in this life or the next, an armchair or a coffee table
might come in handy? The original furniture of the room had simply
disappeared under the slow accumulation of end tables, bureaus, boxes
of china, and photographs. Whole sets of dining-room tables and chairs,
their legs wrapped like the legs of thoroughbreds, pawed the ceiling.
It seemed to me that the tombs of the pharaohs were not more
prudently furnished for the journey into darkness than Grandmother's
nightly resting place.

"Here, in this room," I whispered, "the rich doctor found his wife
hanging from a chandelier."

In the friendly darkness that summer, I told my five listeners how
my sister and I had once slept in that room. We lay in the dark under
the skyline of furniture, chilled by the November breeze that breathed
on us through a tiny window that opened on the garage where Grandmother's ghostly Studebaker stood; it had not been driven for twenty
years. The window was broken. Grandmother had mended it with a
piece of cardboard.

"We were just dropping off to sleep," I said, "when we felt
somebody lift the bed beneath us."

I paused and lowered my voice.

"The furniture began to shake. We felt evil eyes lurking in the dark. Then suddenly, we saw a woman, misty and blue-gray, come through that window, in a horizontal position, and lean over us. There was blood on her neck, and she was weeping. I felt her cold hands on my throat and screamed."

I paused again.

"It was the last time anybody ever slept in that room," I said.

For several nights it looked as though it was the last time anybody would sleep in our bunk room either. Fiction became fact; I almost believed the story myself. And fiction it was—not the house, but the ghost. I'd borrowed it from a book of stories about ghosts in English houses, and none of my listeners was ever the wiser. Here is my source, the original story as it appeared in John H. Ingram's *The Haunted Homes and Family Traditions of Great Britain*:

> Willington is a hamlet, lying in a deep valley between Newcastle-on-Tyne and North Shields. Thirty years ago it consisted of a parsonage, some few cottages, a mill, and the miller's house. The mill is, or was thirty years ago, a large steam flour-mill, like a factory, and near it, but completely detached, was the miller's house. Messrs. Unthank and Proctor were the proprietors and workers of the mill, and Mr. Joseph Proctor, one of the partners, resided in the house adjoining it. . . .
>
> The house . . . was built about the beginning of the present century and, as described by Mr. Howitt in 1847, had nothing spectral in its appearance, although located in a somewhat wild-looking region, just off the river Tyne. The railway runs close by it, and engines connected with coal mines are constantly at work in its vicinity.[2]

Ghost stories, as told by people who tell them to convince you they are true, are often grounded in local history, loaded with dates and the names of witnesses who vow they are skeptics and ignorant of ghosts. Writers of literary ghost stories often borrow this scrupulous attention to time and place; a railroad schedule could not be more accurate than these narrators. They look at their watches and recall the most minute changes in the light and weather, determined to prove what cannot be proved. When Daniel Defoe, whose fictional *Journal of the Plague Year* seems more authentic than his historical sources, wrote "A True Relation of the Apparition of one Mrs. Veal," he must have found it a challenge to write a ghost story based on firsthand testimony that is as matter-of-fact as an item on the social page of a newspaper: Mrs. Veal pays a visit to her friend Mrs. Bargrave, and their conversation is recorded. Only after the visit does Mrs. Bargrave discover that Mrs. Veal has just died in another town and that she has been chatting with a ghost.

But now that we have got past the local history in our story, let us go to the two young ladies who, while visiting Mr. Proctor, were annoyed by the resident ghost. Mr. Howitt received the following account of their experience:

> The first night, as they were sleeping in the same bed, they felt the bed lifted up beneath them. Of course they were much alarmed. They feared lest someone had concealed himself there for the purpose of robbery. They gave an alarm, search was made, but nothing was found. On another night their bed was violently shaken, and the curtains suddenly hoisted up all round the very tester, as if pulled by chords [sic], and as rapidly let down again, several times. Search again produced no evidence of the cause. The next

day they had the curtains totally removed from the bed, re-
solving to sleep without them, as they felt as though evil
eyes were lurking behind them. The consequences of this,
however, were still more striking and terrific. The following
night, as they happened to awake, and the chamber was
light enough—for it was summer—to see everything in it,
they both saw a female figure, of a misty substance and
bluish-grey hue, come out of the wall at the bed's head, and
through the head-board, in a horizontal position, and lean
over them. They saw it most distinctly. They saw it, as a
female figure, come out of, and again pass into, the wall.
Their terror became intense, and one of the sisters, from
that night, refused to sleep any more in the house, but took
refuge in the house of the foreman during her stay, the
other shifting her quarters to another part of the house.[3]

There are two kinds of ghost stories. The first kind includes those
that people tell one another which they claim to be true. Such stories
are rich material for the student of folklore. The second kind is the
literary ghost story, fiction that asks of you only a willing suspension
of disbelief. It should surprise nobody to learn that masters of the
literary ghost story often draw their inspiration from the stories of the
first sort—the tales that people tell one another when they gather
around the fire on a stormy night. Read or hear a few of these and
you come away awed by the variety of ways the dead appear to us.
Some return as gauzy specters, some as moving lights; some are invisible
or arrive in reduced circumstances: a floating head, a skull, a footstep,
a cry. Some climb into their corpses to teach or terrify the living.
Some arrive so intact we mistake them for the living. Only the writer

brought up on cheap horror movies creates ghosts who do nothing but rattle chains. In the folklore of ghosts, they groan, cry, scream, yell, moan, whisper, cough, and clap; they hammer, saw, clink glasses, rattle dice, give parties, eat, drink, smoke, and pull the bedclothes from sleepers. They play violins, pianos, accordions; whole orchestras of ghosts have entertained the living. In the houses we call haunted, they bang doors and shutters on windless nights, make the floors creak, and set up all sorts of noises in the attic. Chairs rock, lights go on by themselves. In churches, ghostly priests say the masses for which they have been paid. In yards, ghostly dogs growl, ghostly cats howl, ghostly cows moo. On the road, the hoofbeats of ghostly horses pound through the night till a ghostly train passes through the countryside and muffles all sound in its wake. And though the dead are often indifferent to us, returning for their own mysterious reasons, my heart goes out to the young woman in one story, a suicide, who every night crawls dripping out of a swimming pool and stands by the bed of her sister and her brother-in-law, the man who rejected her. She tosses her wet hair and on the way out draws it carefully over their faces.

Terrifying, astonishing, poignant—but far removed from the literary ghost story. The recitation of marvels appeals to our curiosity, not our terror. Henry James, the grand old man of the genre, loved marvels as well as the next writer but did not mistake these marvels for stories. "The main condition of interest—that of some appreciable rendering of sought effects—is absent from them," he observes, "so that when, as often happens, one is asked how one 'likes' such and such a 'story' one can but point responsively to the lack of material for a judgement."[4]

Here is the "germ" for that masterpiece of all ghost stories, *The Turn of the Screw:*

Saturday, January 12th, 1895. Note here the ghost-story told me at Addington (evening of Thursday 10th), by the Archbishop of Canterbury: the mere vague, undetailed, faint sketch of it—being all he had been told (very badly and imperfectly), by a lady who had no art of relation, and no clearness: the story of the young children (indefinite number and age) left to the care of servants in an old country-house, through the death, presumably, of parents. The servants, wicked and depraved, corrupt and deprave the children; the children are bad, full of evil, to a sinister degree. The servants *die* (the story vague about the way of it) and their apparitions, figures, return to haunt the house *and* children, to whom they seem to beckon, whom they invite and solicit, from across dangerous places, the deep ditch of a sunk fence, etc.—so that the children may destroy themselves, lose themselves, by responding, by getting into their power. So long as the children are kept from them, they are not lost; but they try and try and try, these evil presences, to get hold of them. It is a question of the children "coming over to where they are." It is all obscure and imperfect, the picture, the story, but there is a suggestion of strangely gruesome effect in it. The story is to be told—tolerably obviously—by an outside spectator, observer.[5]

The "germ" and what James made of it are like the difference between the blurb on a book and the book itself. "Good ghosts, speaking by the book, make poor subjects," he notes in his preface to the collection in which this tale appears. His ghosts, Peter Quint and Miss Jessel, are closer kin with demons than with the mischievous apparitions of traditional ghost lore. "Only make the reader's general vision of evil intense enough . . . and his own experience, his own imagination . . . will supply him quite sufficiently with all the particulars. Make him think the evil, make him think it for himself, and you are released from weak specifications."[6]

Not the ghost but our fear of meeting one terrifies us, a fear realized through the smallest changes in the commonplace. The creak in the floorboard, the light in the window, the shutter banging on a windless night. The strange spirits that intrude themselves upon Ebenezer Scrooge are far less frightening than Marley's ghost and the awful transformation of his door knocker into his dead partner's face, in the opening pages of *A Christmas Carol:*

> Marley's face. It was not in impenetrable shadow, as the other objects in the yard were, but had a dismal light about it, like a bad lobster in a dark cellar. It was not angry or ferocious, but looked at Scrooge as Marley used to look, with ghostly spectacles turned up on its ghostly fore-head. . . .
>
> As Scrooge looked fixedly at this phenomenon, it was a knocker again.[7]

Nobody knew better than my mother the terrors of the commonplace, and one of her pranks has given me the image of how the writer of ghost stories works on his reader. When my mother chose to frighten a houseguest out of his wits, she did so for the same reason that Marley visited Scrooge: to make him a better human being. Her victim was the seven-year-old son of friends of our family. All day long from dawn till dark he boasted that he was afraid of nothing. He teased my sister and me when we confessed that we were afraid of the dark space under our beds. Neither ghost nor ghoul, he assured us, would raise a hair on his head. He would shout at it, fire his cap gun at it; he would scare it to death.

We shall see about that, said my mother to herself. Before he retired for the night, she crept into his room and crawled under the bed. She heard his mother tuck him in, she heard him draw up the covers. Just as he was drifting off to sleep she put her hand under the mattress and lifted it. Once, twice. She felt his whole body stiffen with terror. With a shriek he sprang out and fled howling into the hall. In the tumult of people groping for light switches and bathrobes, my mother made her escape. Needless to say, the boy was cured of his boasting for as long as we knew him. And nobody believed that a ghost had really tried to throw him out of bed.

That's the way with ghosts. One person's testimony is another person's amusement.

The writer of ghost stories is the great illusionist hiding under the bed, making the smallest adjustments in the ordinary, bringing our fears to life. He must be both magician and craftsman, a carpenter of the invisible.

"It is not enough to believe in ghosts, or even to have seen one, to write a good ghost story," observed Edith Wharton. "The greater the improbability to be overcome the more studied must be the approach, the more perfectly maintained the air of naturalness, the easy assumption that things are always likely to happen in that way." Too many horrors spoil the story: "Quiet iteration is far more racking than diversified assaults; the expected is more frightful than the unforeseen."[8]

But how can a writer make the improbable appear to be natural? When an interviewer pointed out to García Márquez that his detailed descriptions of the most fantastic events in *One Hundred Years of Solitude* give them their own reality, he said:

> That's a journalistic trick which you can also apply to literature. For example, if you say that there are elephants flying in the sky, people are not going to believe you. But if you say that there are four hundred and twenty-five elephants in the sky, people will probably believe you. . . . That's exactly the technique my grandmother used. . . . When I was very small there was an electrician who came to the house. . . . My grandmother used to say that every time this man came around, he would leave the house full of butterflies. But when I was writing this, I discovered that if I didn't say the butterflies were yellow, people would not believe it. . . . The problem for every writer is credibility. Anybody can write anything so long as it's believed."[9]

The ghost story that terrifies relies on the dramatic presentation of the situation rather than the creation of complex characters, even when it is told by a narrator. "Dramatise, dramatise," James urges himself, over and over, when mulling over an idea in his notebooks. The characters in the classical ghost story are often types rather than real personalities, and the conventions of the genre can deteriorate into stereotypes in the hands of an unskilled writer. Countless ghost stories open with the cozy scene of guests at a party gathered around the fire, begging one of their number to tell a story. Here is the opening sentence of *The Turn of the Screw:* "The story had held us, round the fire, sufficiently breathless, but except the obvious remark that it was gruesome, as on Christmas Eve in an old house a strange tale should essentially be, I remember no comment uttered till somebody happened to note it as the only case he had met in which such a visitation had fallen on a child."

One of the guests offers to top this story by telling one in which two ghosts visit two children. But it's not his story to tell. "The story's written," he explains. "It's in a locked drawer—it has not been out for years. I could write to my man and enclose the key; he could send down the packet as he finds it." When asked if the story is his, he answers, "Oh thank God, no!" The woman who recorded the story had been dead twenty years.[10]

So what James gives us is a story three times removed: written by a woman, read aloud by a man, and heard by the author himself. Thus the characters are kept at a distance, so that we can give ourselves wholly over to the situation, the better to frighten us. What frightens us, of course, is the authenticity of the governess's story, with its local-color descriptions of Bly and her terrible certainty that she is haunted and her pupils are possessed. If she had told the story directly to Henry James, he would have asked her the kind of skeptical questions literary critics have been asking since the tale was first published. Since she is beyond the grave herself, he (and we as listeners) must accept the mysterious incidents and characters as reported. It's the distance that chills, not simply the situation.

Surely nothing could be more chilling than the situation Robert Frost presents in "The Witch of Coös." The skeleton of a man buried in the cellar pays a visit to the husband and wife who put him there. They entice it to the attic, shut the door, and push the headboard of their bed against it, and ask themselves, "Was there anything up attic that we'd ever want again." Yet because Frost develops the character of the wife, showing us the homely details of her domestic

routine, the tale hangs not on terror but on the human comedy and
her relationship to Toffile, her husband:

> The only fault my husband found with me—
> I went to sleep before I went to bed,
> Especially in winter when the bed
> Might just as well be ice and the clothes snow.
> The night the bones came up the cellar stairs
> Toffile had gone to bed alone and left me,
> But left an open door to cool the room off
> So as to sort of turn me out of it.
> I was just coming to myself enough
> To wonder where the cold was coming from,
> When I heard Toffile upstairs in the bedroom
> And thought I heard him downstairs in the cellar.
> The board we had laid down to walk dry-shod on
> When there was water in the cellar in spring
> Struck the hard cellar bottom. And then someone
> Began the stairs, two footsteps for each step,
> The way a man with one leg and a crutch,
> Or a little child, comes up. It wasn't Toffile:
> It wasn't anyone who could be there.
>
> . . . .
>
> It was the bones. I knew them—and good reason.
> My first impulse was to get to the knob
> And hold the door. But the bones didn't try
> The door; they halted helpless on the landing,
> Waiting for things to happen in their favor.
> The faintest restless rustling ran all through them.

I never could have done the thing I did
If the wish hadn't been too strong in me
To see how they were mounted for this walk.
I had a vision of them put together
Not like a man, but like a chandelier.
So suddenly I flung the door wide on him.
A moment he stood balancing with emotion,
And all but lost himself. (A tongue of fire
Flashed out and licked along his upper teeth.
Smoke rolled inside the sockets of his eyes.)
Then he came at me with one hand outstretched,
The way he did in life once; but this time
I struck the hand off brittle on the floor,
And fell back from him on the floor myself.
The finger-pieces slid in all directions.
(Where did I see one of those pieces lately?
Hand me my button box—it must be there.)[11]

The incident makes us shiver, but afterward, as with Henry James's stories, we come back to wonder and probe as well. How far can we believe the Witch of Coös? Did Toffile really murder her lover? Did she really see the bones (Toffile never does) and lead them into the attic, or did she just want Toffile to think she did, so she can remind him of her lover's bones behind their bed at night? She offers tangible proof that her story is true, but how much faith can be put in a bone in a button-box? The rich ambiguity of the story is such that Randall Jarrell called it the best thing of its kind since Chaucer.

The "Witch" is a supremely gifted storyteller. Despite the occasional gothic touches—the tongue of fire and the smoke rolling out the eye sockets—she tells her adventure in the matter-of-fact way she would use to describe a neighbor's visit. She is a little like García Márquez's grandmother, as he describes her in the interview already quoted. "She told things that sounded supernatural and fantastic, but she told them with complete naturalness. . . . What was most important was the expression she had on her face. She did not change her expression at all," Márquez explained. "In previous attempts to write *One Hundred Years of Solitude*, I tried to tell the story without believing in it. I discovered that what I had to do was believe . . . and write . . . with the same expression . . . : a brick face."[12]

We learn the brick face of belief during our earliest years, when the boundary between real and unreal is blurred. In the epigraph to this chapter, Shelley recalls his desire to commune not with a terrible ghost but with another kind of spiritual being, the guardian spirits of traditional fairy tales, the mysterious old men and women who may or may not be the spirits of the dead. They put the hero on the right road, warn him or her of the dangers to be faced, and offer the means to overcome them. The spirits that Marley sends to visit Scrooge are nothing less than such magic guardians, and James might have been describing *A Christmas Carol* instead of *The Turn of the Screw* when he wrote, "I am prepared with the confession that the 'ghost-story,' as we for convenience call it, has ever been for me the most possible form of the fairy tale."[13] Perhaps it's this link with the fairy tale that in the past made the ghost story especially popular at Christmas; Dickens had an eager audience for his annual Christmas ghost story, and closer to our own time, Robertson Davies's *High Spirits* is a harvest of the stories he wrote for friends and colleagues at Massey College, in the University of Toronto. *The Turn of the Screw* is a story told at a Christmas party at an English country house. Why Christmas rather than Hallowe'en? Because the time of the year before Christmas belongs to the winter solstice, the season of darkness when the living share the countryside with goblins and the spirits of the dead.

When I included the spirits of the dead as characters in my novel *Things Invisible to See* (1985), I drew my inspiration from spirits that members of my family saw—or thought they saw. And if anyone should ask me, Are the spirits real? I must take refuge in Robertson Davies's reply to a similar question: "I believe in them precisely as Shakespeare believed in them." Banquo and Hamlet's father rise from the shadows of art rather than superstition. Davies invokes the wise skepticism of Samuel Johnson: " 'It is wonderful that five thousand years have now elapsed since the creation of the world, and still it is undecided whether or not there has ever been an instance of the spirit of any person appearing after death. All argument is against it, but all belief is for it.' "[14]

In my novel, I call my heroine's guardian spirit the Ancestress, and I credit one of my aunts with introducing me to her. When my Aunt Bon was fifteen, a burst appendix brought her quite literally to death's door. But it was not a door, she told everyone later. It was a river, across which she saw a multitude of relatives nodding at her, all of whom she knew to be dead, many of whom had died before she was born. They called her to join them but she declined, deferring her departure till the age of eighty-one. My aunt's dream, with its mysterious geography, has stayed with me as if it were my own. So many stories start with the question, What if? What if one of these ancestors crossed the river and joined the living? In myths and fairy tales, the guardian spirits—and yes, even the ancient gods—walked among the living to test their courage, to advise them, and to reward them. The character of the Ancestress in my novel is one answer to that question.

Not long after my grandmother died, ending a long convalescence in our house, my mother woke from a deep sleep, perplexed; somebody was drawing a cover over her. She looked up to see her own mother, in a long nightgown, two silvery braids over her shoulders. What would a psychiatrist make of my aunt's dream and my mother's visitation? Jung was no stranger to visions and to dreams that are a sign of our own spiritual healing after illness or grief. Nor is anyone who has been nurtured on fairy tales—or the Bible. Who but a heavenly spirit could warn a poor carpenter and his family to flee into Egypt? Even for the rest of mankind, dreams do not simply show us what we know. They tell us more than we know; they remind us there are many ways of knowing.

But for the writer, knowing is showing. And when I wrote about the Ancestress, though she was invisible to most of the characters, I knew she could not be invisible to the reader. And I tried to record the visits from the Ancestress as concretely as if I were recording a visit from our next-door neighbor: the sounds, the smell, the sight of her who is without earthly substance.

In the fairy tale, in mythology, we meet the dead on an equal footing. Their world is the dark side of ours; indeed, the living may wander into it by accident or design. When Odysseus speaks with the shades in Hades, when Orpheus goes after Eurydice, it is the living who have come to haunt the dead. And what the living find there is as varied as the beliefs of the people who hold them. When the Nigerian novelist Amos Tutuola sends the hero of *The Palm-Wine Drinkard* to bring back his palm-wine tapster from the dead, he finds himself in a land of monsters and magicians, whom he can control with his own magic spells. But closer to our real fears about death is the story from the Nisqualli tribe of southern Washington that tells of a girl whose father marries her off to a rich bridegroom, unaware that the groom and his relatives are all ghosts. At night she arrives in the land of the ghosts with her new family and is greeted by a lively group of people playing games and making merry. She mistakes the dead for the living until she wakes up the next morning:

> The sun was already high in the sky, but not a sound greeted her. She thought this odd, recalling the crowds of people she had seen the night before, and turned to look at her husband, whose head rested on her arm. To her horror she found herself gazing into the empty sockets of a grinning skull. . . .
>
> Without moving her arm she raised herself on her elbow and peered about. The rows of sleeping children were now rows of whitened bones. . . . The bedding that had been so fine was now dirty and old and worn to shreds. . . . Slowly, carefully, she moved her arm until it was free, and as the skull slipped from the crook of her elbow it dropped upon the blanket and turned on its side. . . . Strewn about in groups were endless numbers of skeletons—bones, everywhere bones . . . in all sorts of positions and still at the various games the people had been playing when daylight had overtaken them.[15]

The fear at the heart of the ghost story is the fear of meeting our own fate; shall we not all, in the end, lie down in darkness and leave nothing behind but our bones? When I was a child, I used the word *spooky* to mean "terrifying." I used it, for example, to describe my encounter in a dark church one night before a Christmas pageant in which I was to play an angel. All evening the sanctuary was alive with shepherds, Wise Men, and angels great and small. One by one, the children had been picked up by their parents, and I was left alone to wait for my father while Miss Blaine, the Sunday-school teacher, turned off the lights. I stood barefoot on the stone floor before the altar in my cardboard wings and thin white gown, waiting. Both of us had unsteady nerves. Neither of us knew that sickness would keep me out of the pageant and out of school for a month. Neither of us knew that Miss Blaine was on the verge of a nervous breakdown that would send her to an institution for a long recovery. A ghastly light from the street filtered in through the dark windows, which at this hour showed me none of the friendly saints whose company I enjoyed on Sunday mornings.

Suddenly Miss Blaine took my hand. "Cold hands," she observed. "I love little girls with cold hands."

In that moment she seemed to me a ghost come from the grave to take me with her, acknowledging that I, with my cold hands, was a willing victim. The cold floor, the darkness, the unsettling presence of a woman on the verge of madness—these natural phenomena I erroneously called spooky. I would not call them so today. When I finally came to write of ghosts in *Things Invisible to See,* they were friendly to the living and gave to the everyday a spiritual dimension. The stories that the dead tell and that we tell of the dead make life more glamorous, more intense, and more joyful. Go forth and find your own ghosts; listen and find your own stories.

NOTES

[1] Percy Bysshe Shelley, "A Hymn to Intellectual Beauty," *Shelley's Poetry and Prose* (New York: W. W. Norton & Company, 1977), 95.

[2] John H. Ingram, *The Haunted Homes and Family Traditions of Great Britain* (London: Reeves and Turner, 1912), 266–67.

[3] Ibid., 275.

[4] Henry James, *The Altar of the Dead* (London: Macmillan and Co., Limited, 1992), xx, 3.

[5] *The Notebooks of Henry James,* F. O. Matthiessen and Kenneth B. Murdock, eds. (Chicago: The University of Chicago Press, 1974), 178–79.

[6] Henry James, *A Casebook on Henry James's The Turn of the Screw,* Gerald Willen, ed. (New York: Thomas Y. Crowell Company, 1960), 101.

[7] Charles Dickens, *A Christmas Carol,* in *Charles Dickens's Christmas Tales* (New York: Bonanza Books, 1985), 72.

[8] Edith Wharton, *The Writing of Fiction* (London: Charles Scribner's Sons, 1925), 37, 39–40.

[9] Peter H. Stone, "The Art of Fiction, LXIX," interview with Gabriel García Márquez, *The Paris Review* 82 (Winter 1981): 56.

[10] Henry James, *Henry James: Stories of the Supernatural,* Leon Edel, ed. (New York: Taplinger Publishing Company, Inc., 1970), 437.

[11] Robert Frost, "The Witch of Coös," *The Poetry of Robert Frost,* Edward Connery Lathem, ed. (New York: Holt, Rhinehart and Winston, 1969), 203–5.

[12] Stone, 56.

[13] James, *The Altar of the Dead,* xix.

[14] Robertson Davies, *High Spirits* (New York: Penguin Books, 1982), 5.

[15] John Bierhorst, ed., *The Girl Who Married a Ghost* (New York: Four Winds Press, 1978), 11–12.

THE WATCHER

. . . .

If I could gather together all the lies I told as a child, I think none of them would equal the lie I was told at the funeral of Professor Rubel, a colleague of my father's. Before I tell you the lie, I have to tell you the truth. Like my father, Professor Rubel was a scientist. Unlike my father, he was dying of cancer. He was also very fond of children and had none of his own. When my father visited Professor Rubel for the last time, he took me with him.

Entering the hospital room, I thought the professor must have fallen on hard times, for he did not wear a suit like other men, nor even a lab coat like my father. Professor Rubel greeted us in a gown that barely reached to his knees; he looked like an angel who has been issued the wrong robe. It was October, and a flock of wild geese wrote a ragged *V* on the overcast sky.

"It is wonderful what I can see from this window," remarked Professor Rubel.

A month later I saw him again, in his coffin. Professor Rubel appeared to be sleeping. I do not remember the details of the funeral, which I attended only because the baby-sitter failed to appear. But I do remember the minister's message on that occasion. And this was the message: Professor Rubel was not dead but sleeping. He had fallen asleep in the Lord.

I waited for him to step out of the coffin, and when he did not, I asked my mother why he did not jump up at once, before the coffin was lowered into the earth.

"He's not going to wake *here,*" explained my mother. "He will wake in Heaven."

"But how will he get out of the ground?"

"When you wake in Heaven," said my mother, "you leave your body behind, like baggage."

Why didn't I ask how the soul got to heaven? Because the word *baggage* gave me an answer. I had once seen a coffin being loaded into the baggage car of a train, like the case of a gigantic musical instrument. No doubt people got to heaven by train, a special train for sleepers who woke in a different place and a different condition. Did other sleepers ride it also when they embarked for the less perilous countries of their dreams? And did the conductors ever make mistakes and send to Heaven one whose time had not yet come? Surely this was the danger to which the prayer I said every night made a veiled reference:

Now I lay me down to sleep.
I pray the Lord my soul to keep.
If I should die before I wake . . .

From that night on, I fought sleep like a deadly foe, giving in only when I was too tired to keep my eyes open. I needed a higher authority than my mother to set my mind at rest on this matter, and I found it in Miss Brandenberger, the elderly lady who taught the Monday after-school Bible class in the basement of the Presbyterian church. Five other little girls and I were coloring maps of the Holy Land when, between the taking of a red crayon and the putting away of a blue one, I slipped Miss Brandenberger my question.

"Miss Brandenberger, if I forget to say my prayers, will I die before I wake?"

"Certainly not!" she exclaimed.

"The prayer says it could happen: 'If I should die before I wake.' "

The five other girls glanced up in alarm. Miss Brandenberger, determined to quash an epidemic of difficult questions, said, "There is One who watches over you. You know that. The fall of a single sparrow does not escape His loving eye."

She did not say that the one who watched was God, so I supposed it was some heavenly being whom God had assigned to be the watcher. Probably there were many watchers on the train of sleepers, and they separated the living and the dead at a crucial juncture, like Albany or Chicago, when the conductor's voice boomed over the loudspeaker: "All those passengers going to points west will please move to the head cars. Those cars will be taken off this train."

Indeed, I had heard mention of these watchers in a Christmas carol that my uncle Bill liked to sing at family gatherings, "Green

Grow the Rushes, Ho!" My uncle liked the pagan carols best. The heavenly rest and calm of "Silent Night" bored him. He liked the Yule log, the holly and the ivy, the rising of the sun and the running of the deer, and the partridge in a pear tree. Nearly all his favorite carols could be found in our big Christmas-carol book. But his version of "Green Grow the Rushes, Ho!" did not come from a book. He sang it the way he'd heard it as a child:

> Twelve for the twelve apostles,
> Eleven for the eleven that went to Heaven,
> Ten for the Ten Commandments,
> Nine for nine bright shiners,
> Eight for the April rainers,
> Seven for the seven stars in the skies,
> Six for the secret watchers,
> Five for the symbols at your door,
> Four for the Gospel makers,
> Three, three, the rivals,
> Two, two, the lily white boys
> Clothed all in green-o,
> One is one and all alone
> And evermore shall be so!

Six for the secret watchers. Now let me tell you about the time I saw one of the watchers on a train bound for New York. Although I alone saw him, I was not traveling alone. My sister, my mother, two aunts, one uncle, two cousins, and my grandmother boarded the train late one evening in Ann Arbor. We traveled coach. We reclined the seats as far as they would go and dozed fitfully under our coats.

In the middle of the night I climbed over my sleeping family and set out for the bathroom. Every single soul in the car was asleep but me, and the universe felt chilly, the way it must feel to a kitten that has been separated from its littermates.

Every soul? No, not every soul. As I pattered down the aisle, I saw a white hand resting on a coloring book. By a single beam from the reading light overhead, it was coloring a picture of the man in the moon. The moon was purple, the sky around it was green. I glanced at the face above the hand and saw not a child but a grown man in shirtsleeves. He was nearly bald, but he had a heavy black beard. The seat next to him was empty.

The next morning I was afraid I had dreamed him, and I hurried down to see him again. Ah, how changed! The purple moon in the green sky had disappeared. My watcher was swathed in an overcoat and reading the *Wall Street Journal*. But perhaps this was his daytime disguise, just as the constellations are hidden from us at noon. Perhaps, like the thirty-six secret saints in Jewish folklore, he was both a watcher and an ordinary man, even a foolish one, who only came into the fullness of his wisdom when no one was awake or aware of him. For if he was indeed the watcher, where else could I meet him except in a dream? Dreams are the guardians of sleep, Freud tells us, and not its disturbers. And what was the coloring book but his dream book, the book of our journeys and destinations, of which the dream books sold at newsstands and smoke shops are only a pale reflection?

Many years have passed since I saw that hand secretly coloring the moon among the nighttime travelers. I never again saw a watcher, yet I would be glad for the chance to thank him for the gifts he brings me from time to time. I am in no hurry to join those passengers who no longer dream because, like Professor Rubel, they have awakened out of this life. What is a watcher but a latter-day Hermes, that wise and crafty messenger who traveled so freely between the countries of the living and the dead and who led the souls of the ancient Greeks to Hades? The route he took led past the *demios oneiron,* the village of dreams, located between those who live in the present and those whose present has become the past. Only the living dream. The dream is the language through which our past speaks to us.

When a character in my book *The Highest Hit* rejoices that he has met his dead wife in a dream, I hope my readers will understand why the dream is important. The dream is a place where the dead are alive.

> We lose sight of each other, but we find each other again.
> . . . How lucky I am to have dreams! After she died I
> thought I'd never see her again. Last night we were walking
> on the road to our village in Poland, the way it used to be.
> The fields, all wheat and poppies. . . . And then Rachel and
> I had an argument. You know, she was always a heavy
> woman. She died of a heart attack, talking on the tele-
> phone. Just dropped right over. Two hours before she died,
> she wanted a chocolate pudding for lunch. I told her, "You
> can't have that pudding. You got to watch your weight."
> Now every time I see her, she yells at me, "Why didn't you
> let me eat that pudding, seeing as I only had two hours left
> to go?"[1]

But if dreams teach us anything, it is this: that our past is much broader than we can ever imagine. In an article called "Finding Celie's Voice" Alice Walker describes the dream visitors who came to her from places far beyond her immediate experience:

> After I had finished *The Color Purple* and it was winning
> prizes and being attacked, I had several extraordinary

dream-visits from people I knew before they died and from
people who died before I was born, but whose names and
sometimes partial histories I knew. This seemed logical and
right. But then, at my most troubled, I started to dream of
people I'd never heard of and never knew anything about,
except, perhaps, in a general way. These people sometimes
brought advice, always excellent and upbeat, sometimes just
a hug. Once a dark, heavy-set woman who worked in the
fields and had somehow lost the two middle fingers of
her right hand took hold of my hand lovingly, called me
"daughter," and commented supportively on my work. She
was only one of a long line of ancestors who came to visit
and take my hand that night, all apparently slaves, field-
workers, and domestics, who seemed to care about and
want to reassure me. I remembered her distinctly next
morning because I could still feel her plump hand with its
missing fingers gently but firmly holding my own.

Since I am not white and not a man and not really
Western and not a psychiatrist, I get to keep these dreams
for what they mean to me. . . . Since this dream I have
come to believe that only if I am banned from the presence
of the ancestors will I know true grief.[2]

We all have said, "I had an extraordinary dream," when perhaps
we should have said, "An extraordinary dream visited me." Extraordinary because of the comfort and wisdom dreams can bring us. For
the sake of these gifts, the ancient Babylonians had a special ritual
called incubation, or temple sleep. Those who sought inspired dreams
visited the temples of the dream deities and, after offering prayers and
sacrifice, slept in these sacred places. Even the insomniac might go to

a professional dreamer for help. When Alexander the Great became fatally ill in Babylon, it is said that his generals slept for him in the temple of the god Marduk, hoping for a revelation that would show a cure. When I stay up late to finish a poem or a story, I like to think that writers are the spiritual descendants of those who practiced the nocturnal craft of dreaming.

Dreamers are travelers. Consider the Senoi, a group of people who live in the jungles of the central highlands of Malaysia. Each morning a family gathers to discuss the dreams its members have brought back from the night before. When a Senoi boy, for example, describes a dream of falling, he is greeted with questions that start in wonder and end in poetry,[3] questions that we might ask ourselves and that I will certainly ask Professor Rubel if I meet him in a dream.

"Where did you fall to? What did you discover?"

NOTES

[1] Nancy Willard, *The Highest Hit* (San Diego: Harcourt Brace Jovanovich, 1978), 66–67.

[2] Alice Walker, "Finding Celie's Voice," *Ms.*, Dec. 1985: 96.

[3] David Coxhead and Susan Hiller, *Dreams: Visions of the Night* (New York: The Crossroad Publishing Company, 1976), 11.

THE SKIN ON WHAT
WE'VE SAID

· · · · · · · · · ·

And O! but she had stories,
  Though not for the priest's ear,
To keep the soul of man alive,
  Banish age and care,
And being old she put a skin
  On everything she said.
What shall I do for pretty girls
Now my old bawd is dead?[1]

—William Butler Yeats

As if writers were lost sheep, the muse leads us home, prodding us toward those who first told us stories that made us thrill to be human. Take, for example, my Uncle Gus. He was born on a farm in Deep River, Iowa, and though he was really my mother's cousin, I called him Uncle Gus and his wife Aunt Brigit. He worked as a sheriff in Iowa, a trainman in Minnesota, an insurance salesman in Kansas, an undertaker's assistant in California, and a storekeeper in Wisconsin. I never saw his store, but according to the card he'd had printed to advertise it, whatever you could not find at "Shangri-la Specialties in Drowning Bear, Wisconsin," was not worth owning. Perhaps talking with the customers had honed and polished his repertoire, which seemed endless. Who could forget his stories about the autopsies he'd performed in the barn behind the house during the fierce heat of an Iowa summer? Uncle Gus did not stoop to descriptions of blood and guts. No, his autopsy stories hung on a single awful detail: Aunt Brigit closed all the windows on the north side of the house to keep out the stench.

These stories I heard sitting on the front steps of the house Uncle Gus called the "home place" because his grandfather had built it on the land paid for with the savings he'd kept in a sock under his mattress. *Home place* means: even if the land goes out of the family, never forget this is where we come from.

My mother and sister and I stayed at the home place the summer we drove to Iowa from Michigan for a family reunion. I was nine. The front porch was crammed with aunts, uncles, and cousins who had dropped by from the neighboring farms. Behind the house rose a windmill like a giant silver sunflower. Across the road stretched a field of corn; Uncle Gus said the farmhouse that once stood there had been carried away by a tornado so powerful a box of canceled checks swept from the house had turned up in Milwaukee.

There was also a pump in the yard, which gave cold water flavored with iron. When nobody was watching, I'd put my mouth on the spigot while my sister pumped.

The meals were enormous: sides of beef Aunt Brigit had canned, Great-aunt Ruth's rhubarb-strawberry pie, coffee strong enough to unsettle your stomach all day—though Aunt Brigit put a raw egg in the grounds to soften the flavor.

After dinner Uncle Gus's mother, Great-aunt Ruth, played a song called "All the Little Chickens in the Garden" on the parlor organ, and we children drifted out onto the front porch and waited for Uncle Gus to tell a story. He told every story in the first person, and I never doubted his stories were true, even when he told me about the bridge in Drowning Bear where one night a truck hit and killed a farmer crossing in a dark wagon. And later, said Uncle Gus, when he himself was crossing that bridge at twilight, a blinding white light reared up behind his car and followed him. The faster he drove, the closer it came, chasing him at last right up his own driveway.

"When I jumped from my car and ran into the house, the cornfield to the east looked like it was on fire."

He made no mention of hellfire or the devil. What in his telling of the tale made me believe that the farmer in that dark wagon was death incarnate? By what alchemy did the victim of an accident on the bridge turn into a symbol?

I especially liked the stories in which Uncle Gus did all the voices—like the one he told after he'd eaten five slices of Great-aunt Ruth's smoked ham at dinner. He took his time, both eating and telling stories. He spoke at considerable length about how much Father O'Brien at Holy Name loved Kit Kats. He described the church and the ghost that rumbled in the cellar. He told us how his own mother was a stickler for confession, especially at Easter. I hadn't known that about Ruth.

"So I go into the confessional, and I'm about to make my Easter duty when I notice an unfamiliar face behind the shutter.

" 'You're not Father O'Brien,' I say. 'What are you doing here?'

"And the man says, 'I'm the furniture polisher.'

"And I say, 'Well, where's Father O'Brien?'

" 'I couldn't tell you,' he says, 'but if Father O'Brien has heard anything like the stories I've been listening to, he's gone for the police.' "

Years later I found the story of the furniture polisher in a book of Irish jokes. How could I have ever thought it happened to my uncle? Uncle Gus wasn't even Catholic. And I know of half a dozen people who have confronted the white light on a bridge in places as distant from each other as Ann Arbor and Fairbanks. It's an urban legend. Who knows if it really happened to anyone?

But if today my uncle told me the story of the light that chased him across the bridge or the story of the furniture polisher in the confessional, I would willingly suspend my disbelief. I told him, "You should write these stories down. You should be a writer." He smiled and shook his head. Uncle Gus had not the faintest interest in being a writer, though he would certainly have agreed with the advice Grace Paley says she gives her students at the beginning of every writing course: "If you say what's on your mind in the language that comes to you from your parents and your street and your friends, you'll probably say something beautiful."[2]

What would my uncle think of the writing classes I've taken and the fiction workshops I've taught in which I pass on the two nuggets of advice all writers receive, sooner or later: Show, don't tell; and, Write from what you know. Am I teaching my students to write stories, or am I teaching them to become their own best editors? The early Welsh poets learned their craft by apprenticing themselves to the court bard—the writer-in-residence, you might say—who taught them all the forms and measures. The last year of his training, the apprentice was kept in a dark cell and the measures were chanted to him, outside his window, till he knew them by heart.

Rule number one: Show, don't tell.

I first had an inkling of the power of those words when I was in third grade. The most important subject—as far as I was concerned—was the half hour between the Pledge of Allegiance and arithmetic. It was called Show and Tell, and Miss Hancock explained it to us on the first day of class. Students could stand up in front of the class and share something. A hobby, for example. Or a pet.

The pets that came to school for the next two weeks included a boa constrictor from South America, a tarantula from Arizona, an albino tortoise from Minnesota, and a small iguana whose point of origin was never disclosed. On the day I brought my blue parakeet, Woolworth—we had got him for half price when the dime store closed its pet department—I had a few misgivings. Though he was normally a placid bird, Woolworth had one nervous tic: When he felt that life was more than he could bear, he raced up and down his perch in a frenzy. I'd prepared a little speech on the intelligence of parakeets and how easy it was to teach them to talk—though Woolworth had never uttered a word.

On the morning of his visit, I put the cage, covered with a white cloth, on Miss Hancock's desk. During the Pledge of Allegiance, Woolworth was so quiet I thought he might have suffocated. Then I thought what a neat thing it would be to exhibit him, dead, for Show and Tell. Then I felt terrible for thinking it.

". . . with liberty and justice for all," we chorused, and I stepped forward and whisked the cover off Woolworth's cage. He was alive. Lucy Scranton in the front row said in a low voice, "All she's got to show is her old parakeet."

Did I defend Woolworth? No. I poked him surreptitiously but hard with my pencil. As he danced up and down on his perch, flapping his wings, I told the class that Woolworth was no ordinary bird but one specially trained by Arthur Murray. (My Aunt Nell had taken dancing lessons from Arthur Murray.) He could do the samba. He could do the rumba. He was doing them both at that very moment.

I looked at Woolworth. He was sitting perfectly still. So I went back to my speech about how easily parakeets learned to talk.

"Make him talk," said Lucy Scranton.

I told the class that Woolworth was one of the great talking parakeets of all time, but two days before he'd had a stroke that had robbed him of his speech. (This had just happened to an elderly neighbor of ours.) Before that fatal loss, however, he'd told me the story of his life. His first owner was a pirate who was murdered in Florida. I promised to tell them the second installment the next day. Miss Hancock thanked me and said stories were allowed for Show and Tell only if they were true. A true story, she explained, was one that had really happened.

That was the last prop I took to Show and Tell. Instead I told stories about Aunt Nell and her rumba lessons and Uncle Gus and his white light. I always changed the actual events if they didn't sound true enough to be believed. For writers, showing and telling are the same.

Though Miss Hancock distrusted stories, she loved plays, and she directed two of them that year. The first one was a story about Abraham Lincoln and the Gettysburg Address, which called for two leading roles and a whole lot of citizens. Citizen One, Citizen Two, Citizen Three—they didn't have names. I played Citizen Eighteen. Grumblers and malcontents all of us; we wanted bigger parts. The play was a huge success with the parents and the other teachers. Several months after *Lincoln at Gettysburg,* Miss Hancock announced she would be directing us in *The Pied Piper of Hamelin.* At first this seemed an improvement: there was a character called the Mayor and a lot of children, who had names, and their parents, who had occupations. There were also five council members. I felt hopeful until the parts were assigned. I was to play Council Member Five.

I refused. If I couldn't play someone with a real name, I would not be in the play at all. The other four council members took courage and defected also. Miss Hancock rose to the challenge.

"Council Member One, you are the Keeper of the Treasury. Council

Member Two, you are the Town Historian. Council Member Three, you are the Town Librarian. Council Member Four, you are Town Dog Warden. Council Member Five, you are the Keeper of True Stories."

Such was my first title, my first degree, you might say, with all the rights and privileges pertaining thereto. I was not the town story-teller; Miss Hancock did not quite trust the truth of fiction, and perhaps she had never heard of oral history, which preserves so many family stories. Keeper of True Stories was a safe, useful occupation. It would keep me in the play and out of trouble.

But aren't all writers keepers of true stories in one way or another? Perhaps even folktales are family stories that have simply wandered away from their source. Close to the source is Amy Tan, setting down the tales passed on by her mother and her mother's friends in *The Joy Luck Club*. Further away are local legends and ghost stories, whispered in bunk rooms at summer camp after the lights are out.

So often family stories are not heard. They are overheard and repeated at family gatherings until they are as much a part of you as the color of your eyes. When I was growing up, my grandmother lived with us near the end of her life. At mealtimes, she told the same stories over and over—a habit I attributed to her bad memory. It never occurred to me that she was trying to teach me what she knew about who we were and where we'd come from, and these tales would never be mine till I knew them by heart.

Family stories are rarely handed down intact. No, they come to us like pieces of a quilt too good to throw away: an anecdote, an image.

"One of our relatives was portrait painter to the king," my grand-mother used to say.

What king? What court? Where had she got such an idea? Like the message heard by the last person in a game of Telephone, family stories are altered in the hearing and improved in the telling. My mother remembered being told by her mother, "Grandpa came to America in a boat." She naturally assumed it was a rowboat; growing up inland, she'd never seen any other kind. For many years she treasured the image of her grandfather braving the high waves, rounding the coast of Sweden before heading out to the open sea. Who knows how many children heard the story before her father corrected her? I like to imagine those children passing it on to their children, who add to it, change it, and end by claiming my great-grandfather as their own.

A friend of mine in college told me that her own mother once dated a boy whose parents had a passion for genealogy. And because she liked the boy and having respectable ancestors was important to his family, she did not tell him that she was left as an infant on the altar of the Dutch Reformed Church in Wyandotte, Michigan, and found by the pastor, who arranged to adopt her. Instead she went to the local antique store and bought a box of old photographs, named them, dated them, and arranged them in an album. Instant ancestors. Many years later, when I visited my friend the instant ancestors were hanging alongside the pictures of her husband and two children. I said nothing, and neither did she. Both her children bore a strong resemblance to the woman they called their great-grandmother.

Since hers are fictional relatives turned into real ones, my friend will never know the pitfalls of turning real relatives into fictional ones. The first pitfall is the confusion your relatives feel when they find themselves transformed into characters. I think nobody describes this better than Toni Cade Bambara in the preface to her collection of stories *Gorilla, My Love:*

It does no good to write autobiographical fiction cause the minute your book hits the stands here comes your mama screamin how could you and sighin death where is thy sting and she snatches you up out your bed to grill you about what was going down back there in Brooklyn when she was working three jobs and trying to improve the quality of your life and come to find on page 42 that you were messin around with that nasty boy up the block and breaks into sobs and quite naturally your family strolls in all sleepy-eyed to catch the floor show at 5:00 A.M. but as far as your mama is concerned, it is nineteen-forty-and-something and you ain't too grown to have your ass whipped.[3]

Even the most innocuous descriptions can get you into serious trouble. In a story of mine called "Sailing to Cythera" a friendly monster lives undisturbed under the bed of a little boy because nobody ever dusts there. My mother read the story and was appalled. "Everybody in my bridge club will think I don't clean under the beds," she moaned. "They'll think our house is filthy."

More serious—from the writer's point of view—is the shadow real life casts over the writer trying to shape it into a work of fiction. An early draft of my novel *Things Invisible to See* included all sorts of characters who had nothing to do with the main story—an excess my editor was quick to point out. Why, she inquired, were these characters there? It took months for me to find the answer. The germ of the novel was a family story, and I was guided by a hidden obligation to tell the truth— that is, to narrate the events as they happened in real life.

But my novel had a different shape and purpose from the events that inspired it. "Fiction is a lie," Eudora Welty reminds us. "Never in its inside thoughts, always in its outside dress. . . .

"The reason why every word you write in a good novel is a lie, then, is that it is written expressly to serve the purpose; if it does not apply, it is fancy and frivolous, however specially dear to the writer's heart."[4] Only when you've broken the personal connection between you and your material can you free those family stories to wear the livery of art.

Rule number two: Write from what you know.

After I entered junior high, Miss Hancock and her minions seemed like a memory of friendly spirits in the Garden of Eden. Elementary school was noncompetitive; *report card* was a dirty word and *grades* almost as bad. Junior high was the real world, with three-hour final exams in every subject at the end of each semester. The age of innocence was over.

The first week of class, all new students were given placement tests in math and English. In math I did badly. Ironically, it was the story problems that caused my downfall: *From a piece of cloth that measured 691 yards, Jane bought 273 yards. How many yards were left?* How could I possibly answer unless I could unroll the cloth, cut it, and take a yardstick to what remained? To this day, I think story problems are not only frustrating but also disappointing. Here we have a character named Jane who is buying enough cloth to cover three football fields. Who cares about what's left on the bolt? The real question is, What's she planning to do with all that cloth?

Having perused my math test, the examiner concluded I had an IQ below my knees. I was not only put into remedial math but, on the strength of my math exam—or rather the weakness—into remedial English. Three days passed before the examiners got around to reading my English exam and mending the error of their ways. Thank goodness they took their time. What I learned in remedial English will stay with me for the rest of my life.

Picture a small, windowless room with a table and three chairs and a hooked rug. The space was cozy; it used to be a utility closet, and you could still see the hooks where generations of janitors had hung their brooms and buckets. Miss Reilly, the blond, peppy reading specialist, was doing her practice teaching and earning extra credit for tutoring a boy named Derek Johnson and me. All I knew for sure about Derek Johnson was that he lived on a farm outside Ann Arbor, and he wore the same blue-plaid flannel shirt to school every day. Like me he wore glasses. Mine had gold rims and were new. His were flesh-colored plastic; one of the earpieces was taped with black electrical tape.

Miss Reilly took out that awful Dick and Jane reader I had left behind in first grade, opened it to page one, and handed it to Derek Johnson.

"I want you to read for me, Derek," she coaxed.

Derek read "Run . . . Spot . . . run," with long pauses between each word. He nailed each letter with his thumb as if he were killing a noxious insect. Sweat poured down his face.

"That's fine, Derek," she said.

We all knew it wasn't. She handed the book to me.

"Will you start reading where Derek left off?"

Until that moment I'd planned to rattle off the whole reader and to tell her I'd finished *Jane Eyre* just the week before. But how could I do that to Derek Johnson, whose pain suffused the very air around us? So I said, "I can't, Miss Reilly."

"You can't read a single word?" she exclaimed.

I shook my head.

"Derek, can you help her?"

Hope glimmered in his eyes and faded as he turned the page. After a lengthy silence, Miss Reilly said, "Try to sound out the first word. It's a word you know."

"I don't know it," he whispered fiercely, close to tears. "I don't know anything."

Miss Reilly closed the book and tore a sheet of paper from her notebook. She looked ready to cry herself.

"That's not true," she said. "You know a lot. Let's make a list of things you know."

Another silence.

"Your names," she said. "We'll start with your names."

Names. What else did we know? Derek knew how to tell a guernsey from a holstein. I knew the number of sharps in the key of *F*. Derek knew how many wins Bob Feller had earned for Cleveland the year before. I knew the Lord's Prayer in Spanish and the second verse of "The Battle Hymn of the Republic." Derek knew how to find the North Star. I knew how to find the star in an apple.

Did Derek Johnson ever learn to read? I don't know. A Chinese sage once said that when we have seen the ten thousand things in their unity, we go back to the beginning and find ourselves where we have always been. Eudora Welty reminds us that sometimes writers write best about what they know by staying where they know it. "Yet writing of what you know has nothing to do with security: what is more dangerous? How can you go out on a limb if you do not know your own tree?"[5]

When I arrived at Vassar for my first teaching job, fresh from the Midwest, it seemed to me that everyone around me knew more than I did. My colleagues could crack jokes in Greek and Icelandic. They went to the opera on Saturdays. One man played a harpsichord, another the violin. What they hadn't heard or read scarcely seemed worth knowing about. They chattered wisely of Beaujolais and Brie while I listened in awed silence, for I grew up in a house without wine, and the only cheese I knew was what my mother called "store cheese." My father used it to bait his mousetraps.

Oh, I would never catch up with my colleagues. They'd spent the long hours of childhood improving themselves while I played Tarzan and Red Rover in the backyards of Ann Arbor, Michigan, and the back roads of Deep River, Iowa. While my colleagues were being taken to the ballet, I was watching my Aunt Nell practice her rumba lessons in the living room. While they were reading *The Odyssey,* I was listening to my Uncle Gus describe the horrors of performing an autopsy in a barn in one-hundred-degree heat without air-conditioning.

And I'm saying, "Uncle Gus, you should write all this stuff down." And he smiles and shakes his head.

It was a long time before I understood that I did not know less than my colleagues, but that what I knew was entirely different from what they knew. For better or worse, I was a keeper of true stories, and my head was full of voices, for I could never separate stories from the people who told them. "Perhaps the proper measure of a writer's talent is his skill in rendering everyday speech, when it is appropriate to his story," writes Paule Marshall, "as well as his ability to tap, to exploit, the beauty, poetry and wisdom it often contains."[6]

So when I teach writing, I send my students in search of everyday speech. They do interviews, they do oral histories, they listen to voices different from their own. Here, for example, is the voice of a woman—born in Carroll County, Georgia, in 1910—explaining to an interviewer how she met her husband:

> It was just pourin' down rain, and he was goin' some-
> where, and he come up on the porch to get dry. I was in
> the barn milkin', and when I come back to the house I

heard my mother talkin' to him. So I went out there, and Ma told me who it was, and he introduced hisself. Then after it slacked up he started back down the road.

I told my mother, I said, "That's my man!"

She said, "You say that again, I'll whup ya!"

I said, "He's mine!"

She said, "He might be a married man."

I said, "If he is, I'll put a spider in his wife's dumplin's."

Well, after it quit rainin' I went down to this neighbor's house, and I described him up to her.

"That's Buck Moss, all right," she said.

"Is he married?" I said.

"No," she said.

"Well, good," I said. "Then he's mine."

Sure enough, he come back.[7]

This is not a story, but it could certainly be the start of one. You have characters, point of view, plot, and place. Most important, you have the right voice for showing them. And you have a character just itching to tell the story her way. A strong voice will give you a poem or story you didn't think you knew enough to write, if you are willing to follow it.

Here's a different voice—younger, more contemporary. It's from a book called *Bad Dates,* for which a number of celebrities were asked to describe a date that ended in disaster. The speaker is Terry Power, a film and music-video producer:

I was housesitting in an upper-class bedroom community where I had this incredible arrangement—a beautiful house, a Jaguar at my disposal, and a swimming pool. All I had to do was take care of the family dog, make sure the house was safe while the people were away in Europe, and keep an eye on my housemate, Sophie, an older woman whose husband had run off with the high school home-ec teacher, who had taught all of her five children. This drove her to drink.

I never saw Sophie eat a meal. All I saw her consume was vodka, Triscuits and Cheez Whiz. That was it.[8]

If you read no further, you might think you were reading a story about Sophie, though an editor would probably advise the author to open with that last line rather than with *I was housesitting in an upper-class bedroom community*. The journalist tries to give you the facts. The narrative writer tries not to. Part of telling a story well is keeping information back and letting it escape when the time is right. It so happens that Sophie is not the bad date, only the go-between, though as a character Sophie is far more interesting. Very soon we hear no more of Sophie. Power is telling an anecdote—a true one. He is not writing a story.

Some people tell anecdotes for years, and then one day they cross over and tell stories. To borrow a phrase from Yeats, they put a skin on what they say till it is true the way stories are true, not in its outside dress but its inside thoughts. Here is Bob Dylan in an interview from 1966 during which he answers the question, "What made you decide to go the rock-and-roll route?"

Carelessness. I lost my one true love. I started drinking. The first thing I know, I'm in a card game. Then I'm in a crap game. I wake up in a pool hall. Then this big Mexican lady drags me off the table, takes me to Philadelphia. She leaves me alone in her house, and it burns down. I wind up in Phoenix. . . . I start working in a dime store, and move in with a thirteen-year-old girl. Then this big Mexican lady from Philadelphia comes in and burns the house down. I go down to Dallas. I get a job as a "before" in a Charles Atlas "before and after" ad. I move in with a delivery boy who can cook fantastic chili and hot dogs. Then this thirteen-year-old girl from Phoenix comes and burns the house down. The delivery boy—he ain't so mild: he gives her the knife and the next thing I know I'm in Omaha. It's so cold there, by this time I'm robbing my own bicycles and frying my own fish. I stumble onto some luck and get a job as a carburetor out at the hotrod races every Thursday night. I move in with a high-school teacher who also does a little plumbing on the side, who ain't much to look at but who's built a special kind of refrigerator that can turn newspaper into lettuce. Everything's going good until the delivery boy shows up and tries to knife me. Needless to say, he burned the house down, and I hit the road. The first guy that picked me up asked me if I wanted to be a star. What could I say?[9]

Wouldn't all of us rather have Dylan's tall tale than the plain facts of how he embarked on his musical career? I love tall tales because lying is the rule of the game when you tell one, and lying is what writers do best—though we lay our hands on our hearts and swear it's the truth we're telling. Telling a tall tale can be beneficial to your health; it has a liberating effect on your imagination. When I was teaching in Fairbanks, Alaska, I met a young writer who was getting ready to enter the annual tall-tale contest. He wanted to know how hot it gets in New York. "I want to make up a story about heat," he said. "All people talk about here is the cold." I didn't have the heart to say, Write about what you know.

How do the tall-tale spinners talk about the cold? Why, it was so cold the sun went to bed in an overcoat, clutching a load of kindling. The mercury in the thermometer turned blue. The smoke clouds froze over the chimney; we had to chop them off. The fire froze in the fireplace; we had to bury it to darken the room for sleep. A tale close to my heart is one in which a man sees his brother's words freezing in front of his very eyes. "He caught some of them in a sack," says the tale teller, "and carried them home and thawed them out by the fire. His inability to catch them all resulted in a disconnected line of chatter that he could not understand."[10]

Catching the words and carrying them home, not in a sack but in the heart: That's what the keeper of family stories does, and the family includes all of us. No man is an island; we are both keepers and kept, and our stories stitch the living and the dead into a single fabric, a coat to keep us from the winds that blow through the spaces the dead once filled.

Are they true stories? Better to ask, Do they keep the wind out? In one of my favorite stories by Isaac Bashevis Singer, "Gimpel the Fool," the question itself is the answer: "The longer I lived the more I understood that there were really no lies. Whatever doesn't really happen is dreamed at night. It happens to one if it doesn't happen to another, tomorrow if not today, or a century hence if not next year. What difference can it make? Often I heard tales of which I said, 'Now this is a thing that cannot happen.' But before a year had elapsed I heard that it actually had come to pass somewhere."[11]

Two years ago I went back to Deep River for a visit. Great-aunt

Ruth had died at the age of ninety-four. The power lines had come through in the late fifties, and now the families out that way had television and electric stoves and iceboxes. No more drinking straight from the pump in the yard; years of chemical fertilizers had poisoned the earth around the farms in Deep River. Everything had changed. For the first time I noticed how few books there were in Uncle Gus's house. The Bible, an old issue of *Good Housekeeping,* and a hymnal on Aunt Brigit's parlor organ—that was it.

And nothing had changed. In the evening the front porch was packed with aunts, uncles, and cousins, and all of us were older now and wiser and stouter. Everyone had brought photograph albums to show me what I'd missed: a wedding, a graduation, a trip to Wisconsin Dells. Even Kodak does not last forever; the oldest photographs had a pale green cast as if I were seeing them under a skin of water. With the passing of another generation perhaps the images will have faded beyond recognition.

Uncle Gus said, "We have some real nice pictures of our mother if you want to see 'em. We laid her out in the satin dress she wore at the Centennial."

"Of course I want to see them," I said.

"Not everybody likes to see pictures of dead people," said Aunt Brigit, "so I always make Gus ask."

The photographs showed Ruth laid out in a bright blue satin dress and sunbonnet as if she were on her way to a rodeo in heaven.

"She doesn't look ninety-four," I said.

"Never did," said Aunt Brigit.

"She's wearing a beautiful dress," I added.

Aunt Brigit looked pleased. "Made me one just like it," she said.

She glanced up to check on the children playing in the yard. Across the road stretched the cornfield from which, long ago, a farmhouse had been carried off by a tornado. When I was nine, the field seemed to stretch from everlasting to everlasting. Now I could see where it ended. A combine in the northeast acres was harvesting the sheaves, and though darkness was coming on fast, the crisp stalks fell silently, steadily, like an army under fire. In its wake, two horses gleaned what the combine had missed.

"Maybe you want to see Mother's writings," said Gus.

I was astonished. Ruth a writer? When on earth had she found the time? I said of course I wanted to see her writings. Aunt Brigit brought out a shoe box half filled with scraps of paper rolled up and fastened with rubber bands.

"Go ahead. You can unroll 'em," said Uncle Gus.

I unrolled the first scroll, and what looked like a primitive clothespin dropped into my lap. The note accompanying it was written in pencil, but the handwriting was clear:

> This is the old husking peg that Dad fixed smaller to fit my hand when I used to help him husk corn the first year we were married and other years later, when the kids helped husk too, or the smaller ones rode in the wagon. I would get up early and put a chicken in the oil stove oven and have the potatoes peeled and bread all baked ready in the big stone jar in the pantry. Butter churned and canned fruit in basement I could open quick so we could hurry back to the field, then wash all those dishes at night. I made Aunt Annie's nice dresses over for the girls and I made the boys' everyday shirts and coveralls when they were small. Sat up many nights darning stockings and sacks or making comforts to keep everyone warm in the cold

winters. Always was the first one up in the morning and started the fires and got breakfast ready. Those were the happy days when I had all my children near.

"We keep findin' Mother's notes all over the house," said Uncle Gus. "Maybe someday you'll put her in a story."

The paper she'd written on was brittle. It could not last much longer. Was that why he'd shown me her notes, so that I could keep her story alive—at least for the next generation?

From the front yard came a shout: "Here I come, ready or not!" The fields around Deep River were dark now, and the children, hidden, grew quiet as birds in the morning—alert, joyful, listening.

NOTES

[1] William Butler Yeats, "John Kinsella's Lament for Mrs. Mary Moore," in *Selected Poems and Three Plays of William Butler Yeats* (New York: Macmillan, 1962), 195.

[2] Paule Marshall, "The Poet in the Kitchen," interview with Grace Paley, *The New York Times Book Review,* 9 Jan. 1983: 3.

[3] Toni Cade Bambara, *Gorilla, My Love* (New York: Random House/Vintage Books Edition, 1972), ix.

[4] Eudora Welty, "Place in Fiction," in *The Eye of the Story* (New York: Random House, 1977), 119, 121.

[5] Ibid., 130.

[6] Marshall, 3.

[7] Alvin Schwartz, *When I Grew Up Long Ago* (Philadelphia: J. B. Lippincott, 1978), 201.

[8] Carole Markin, *Bad Dates* (New York: Citadel Press, 1990), 178.

[9] Charles Kaiser, "Encountering Dylan," *Boston Review,* April 1986; reprint in *Harper's* magazine, June 1986: 36.

[10] Roger Welsch, *Shingling the Fog and Other Plains Lies* (Chicago: Swallow Press, 1972), 29: reprint from *Nebraska Farmer* (Jan. 3, 1925, Otoe County).

[11] Isaac Bashevis Singer, "Gimpel the Fool," in *An Isaac Bashevis Singer Reader* (New York: Farrar Strauss Giroux, 1971), 20.

LOOKING FOR
MR. AMES

• • • • • • • • •

I was a sophomore at the University of Michigan when I took my first class from Professor Ames. He taught a course called "The Art of Writing." The catalog said, "By Special Permission," but I know of no one who was turned away for lack of skill. Each semester a new crop of stories would attach itself to the lore already surrounding this man.

Fact: He was of slight build yet surprisingly strong; he had twice broken one of the thermal panes in Haven Hall simply by the act of closing the window. At the age of forty he had married one of his students, Madeline Shaw. On their wedding night, which they spent in his tiny bachelor apartment, the new bride thought she had never slept in so uncomfortable a bed in her life. A camel could not have been lumpier. The next morning she lifted up the mattress and discovered the springs were crammed with all the books her new husband had started to read but never got around to finishing.

Fact: He loved toys. Russian nesting dolls, treetop angels, Matchbox Cars. A young woman in Mr. Ames's modern novel class said his office made her feel she was in the waiting room of her orthodontist, who had a shelf filled with amusements for his young patients. The top shelf of Mr. Ames's bookcase held half a dozen Quaker Oats boxes. When you had a conference with Mr. Ames, those good-natured witnesses beamed down at you.

Over this chaos presided a small silver Byzantine Madonna. She hung from a shoelace on the wall behind his desk, and she looked as if she had her blessed hands full. Mr. Ames was not Greek Orthodox, though he sometimes went to Christmas and Easter services at Saint Nicholas and left before the sermon.

Fact: While leading a discussion of a particularly mediocre story, Mr. Ames gave a brilliant extemporaneous lecture on voice in fiction, during which every student understood, in a deep intuitive way, that the universe is holy and that every part is connected to every other part. If a spider entered this classroom and one of us killed it, said Mr. Ames, its death would be felt in the farthest galaxy. Before you pick a rose, you must first ask permission of the stars. His performance quite eclipsed the mediocre story; nobody present at the discussion can recall so much as a single detail.

Rumor: Mr. Ames was supposed to be working on a book about writing and teaching.

Fact: Not a student took his class without wondering if he or she was mentioned in it.

In those days I thought all professors of literature, when left to their own devices, dreamed in metaphor and spoke in epigrams. Tweed jackets with leather patches on the elbows were in fashion, and the air of genteel poverty worn by even the lowliest instructors made a great impression on me. I loved their desks bustling with papers and all the paraphernalia of their profession—blue books and class registers, pipes at rest on giant glass ashtrays, and notes slipped under the door or taped to the frosted glass: "Dear Mr. Ames. I had this great idea for a story but when I wrote it, it wasn't so great. Can I come see you?"

I think it was partly for these things I became a teacher my-self. But my office at Vassar is so small I must step aside to let students get to the chair. I have no pipe (I don't smoke) and no space for my books; those that fill the shelves belong to the two previous occupants, now on leave. The boxes of books lined up on the floor once belonged to Elizabeth Bishop; my officemate is doing extensive research on her work. Gladly do we share our space with her wise spirit.

Clutching the poem I hoped would get me into Mr. Ames's class, I sat on the floor outside his office; the English Department had forsworn the luxury of chairs. Part of my mind listened to the buzz of voices behind closed office doors. The other part reviewed Book Seven of *The Republic* for an exam in my Great Books class: "Wherefore each of you, when his time comes, must go down to the general underground abode, and get in the habit of seeing in the dark. When you have acquired the habit, you will see ten thousand times better than the inhabitants of the den . . . because you have seen the beautiful and just and good in their truth."[1]

Suddenly a door at the end of the corridor opened and a deep voice floated out.

"Listen, I'm telling you the truth. The linoleum at Sears is actually fifty cents cheaper."

There is a theory of knowledge that says we are led to the truth by a series of disillusionments. In my universe, such truth isn't worth knowing. What kept my illusions alive at that moment was Mr. Ames, who opened his door and called me into his office. He wore a white shirt and a tie on which he had spilled—good grief, was it egg? The desk was a glorious confusion of books and papers and empty wrappers of Dutch Girl instant hot chocolate. On the wall behind him hung a plaque that read:

FISHERMAN'S CODE
Early to bed
Early to rise
Fish all day
And make up
    lies.

I read it and glanced back at him.

"That's what writers do," he said.

Speechless, I handed him my poem, written in ultrafree verse. It was called "The Gardener's Song," and today I don't remember a single line. He read it over. He did not say it was wonderful. He said: "I know a poet *you'd* like. Charlotte Mew."

I wrote down the name: *Charlotte Mew*. I had never heard of

Charlotte Mew. Mr. Ames leaned back in his swivel chair, and I realized how short he was. His feet did not even touch the floor.

"Welcome to 'The Art of Writing,' " he said. And he handed me back my poem.

Mr. Ames's class unfolded in a series of cold gray afternoons, the perpetual November of a Michigan winter. I can still see us, fifteen students shuffling into the classroom in parkas and clumpy boots, waiting for Mr. Ames to arrive swathed in the old trench coat he wore winter and spring. Tuesday and Thursday, Tuesday and Thursday, Tuesday and Thursday—very soon we took him for granted, the way we take air and water for granted till the time arrives when we don't have them.

What did I learn from this man? I seem to remember no single insight of any great importance. Yet I know that for all of us there were days when nothing mattered more than what Mr. Ames thought of our newest story, our nearly finished poem. I remember his office but not what we said to each other in that remarkable place. And I remember his voice as he read to us Theodore Roethke's lovely villanelle "The Waking":

> I wake to sleep, and take my waking slow.
> I feel my fate in what I cannot fear.
> I learn by going where I have to go.
>
> We think by feeling. What is there to know?
> I hear my being dance from ear to ear.
> I wake to sleep, and take my waking slow.

Of those so close beside me, which are you?
God bless the Ground! I shall walk softly there,
And learn by going where I have to go.

Light takes the Tree; but who can tell us how?
The lowly worm climbs up a winding stair;
I wake to sleep, and take my waking slow.

Great Nature has another thing to do
To you and me; so take the lively air,
And, lovely, learn by going where to go.

This shaking keeps me steady. I should know.
What falls away is always. And is near.
I wake to sleep, and take my waking slow.
I learn by going where I have to go.[2]

Rumor: Mr. Ames was a student of Roethke's at Michigan State in a class that had passed from history into legend. The building in which the class met had windows on three sides. One fateful day Roethke told his students he wanted them to describe a physical action. "Now you watch what I do for the next five minutes and describe it," he said, whereupon he opened a window, climbed out on the narrow ledge of the building, and inched around the three sides, all the while making faces at the students through the glass. The girl who told me Mr. Ames's office reminded her of her orthodontist's waiting room also told me this, so perhaps she was not a reliable source.

And I remember some of the poems Mr. Ames asked us to

memorize. We had to learn a new one every other week. You could choose your own, and you could recite it or write it out in class, but you had to know it. This was a task after my own heart, for who knew when I might find myself in a place without books? I loved to dwell in the cool high rooms of the public library on Washington Street, the dark crowded rooms of the secondhand bookshops along State and Liberty. I could not imagine life without books.

Three years earlier, the summer I turned sixteen, my family moved from Ann Arbor, Michigan, to Los Alamos, New Mexico, and I felt as if we were moving from the civilized world to the moon. "The desert is beautiful," my father told me. What was the desert to me? I wanted to hear him say, "The public library is even better than the one in Ann Arbor."

I packed my Emily Dickinson and my Blake, my *Songs and Sonnets of Shakespeare,* and a book with the rather presumptuous title *One Hundred Great Modern Poems.* I was sixteen, and I wanted to get poetry into my head so that even in the desert I could say to myself, My mind to me a kingdom is. And in the middle of the atomic city, while horned toads basked on our patio, I memorized a poem a week.

Now, years later, I find that though I have forgotten many of the words to the poems, I have not forgotten their music or what Frost called the sound of sense. And I have come to believe that one of the most valuable things a writer can do is to memorize poems and passages that he wishes he'd written himself.

Of my Blake-to-Keats class with Mr. Ames, I remember a few of the poems I learned by heart, fewer insights, and no dates. But I have not forgotten his voice as he read aloud to us. It rises up clearly behind the familiar words. Will my voice carry that far? I read poems aloud to my students and urge them to read their own work to one another. Nothing so quickly reveals the ill-turned phrase or the sentence staggering under the weight of too many adjectives as reading your own work out loud.

Not long after graduation I dreamed I had stumbled into a secondhand shop presided over by an angel. The angel led me down aisles crammed with pedestals, wings, dolls, hair nets, chairs, garbage cans, flowerpots, feathers, gloves.

"Nothing is for sale," the angel explained. "It all belongs together. Listen, can you hear it?"

I listened.

"I hear a heartbeat," I said.

The angel smiled. "That's the poetry of things. Isn't it wonderful? The universe scans."

After I left Ann Arbor, I lost touch with Mr. Ames, except for the cards I addressed at Christmas to him and to his wife, and the cards they sent me in return. The note at the bottom was always in Madeline's handwriting and one of them said how pleased her husband was to see my poems beginning to appear in the quarterlies. I was surprised and comforted to know that Mr. Ames was still aware of me: two stars, one large, one small, both dancing in the same galaxy.

It is odd how news of great events so often arrives in a whisper. Browsing in a Barnes & Noble on Fifth Avenue, I ran into the man who'd sat two rows behind me in Mr. Ames's writing class. He looked as if he were made up to play the part of a successful middle-aged broker. I don't know what he thought of me; time had written new parts for us both.

"I wonder if Mr. Ames still has those oatmeal boxes in his office," I said.

"You haven't heard? He had an operation to remove a tumor in his stomach. I heard it was cancer. I hope they got all of it."

Several months later I was in Ann Arbor for a Fourth of July family reunion. I called Mr. Ames at home and reached Madeline. The last time I'd spoken with her, years before, I had stopped by the house to deliver a late paper. Now in my mind's eye I saw her clearly: a slender woman with blond braids coiled at the nape of her neck. Her husband was still teaching, she said, though he'd taught the last five classes of the semester from a hospital bed.

"I'm sure he'd be glad to see you. He's in Room Thirty. I'll be going back to the hospital right after lunch if you'd like a ride."

I thanked her and said that I couldn't get away till late afternoon. On a summer's day the one-mile walk from my mother's house to the hospital seemed to take no more than a few minutes. Dylan Thomas once said he liked to think of poetry as statements made on the way to the grave. Appropriate, I thought, that the walk to the hospital took me past Forest Hills Cemetery. The wrought-iron gate always stands open. From the street you can see, just beyond the rise in the gravel path, a magnificent stone angel, bigger than life—though I suppose that even when they are not magnificent, angels are always bigger than life.

When I arrived at the hospital, I had completely forgotten the number of Mr. Ames's room. The receptionist scanned a chart on the wall and said, "He's been moved to intensive care. Are you family?"

"No, but his wife is expecting me."

"You'll need a pass," said the receptionist, and handed me a well-worn strip of cardboard, numbered 2.

Fact: The door to intensive care is marked Authorized Personnel Only, and the whole wing is as cool and still as the opening of a rose. I peeked into the first room beyond that door. The man in the bed, connected by tubes to a monitor and an IV bag, was certainly Mr. Ames, though in an edited, sallower version, as if an evil spell had

diminished him. His wife sat on the edge of his bed. They were laughing together; she was waving her hands, telling him a story.

I knocked, and they both looked up.

"Good morning," I said, and remembered it was the middle of the afternoon.

Mr. Ames's face broke into a smile. He was still Mr. Ames, but he was dying. Madeline stood up and said she was going to sneak off for a cup of coffee. I felt as tongue-tied as on that distant day I'd stopped by his office and handed him the poem that would be my passport into his course.

"How are you?" I asked lamely.

"Since you're here, I'm almost well, at least for the time being."

Seeing that I could hardly utter a word, he began to talk about his students. This one had just published a poem in *The Virginia Quarterly Review*—did I remember her? She sat in the back row of our class. That one had given up writing and entered Yale Divinity School. Mr. Ames knew all of us by name. He knew what we had done with our lives, and he knew what our lives had done with us.

"How do you remember us all?" I asked.

He chuckled.

"It's easier to remember you than to forget you. My great-aunt taught fourth grade for forty years. The last five years of her life she had Alzheimer's. She stayed in her room at the nursing home and spent her days scolding forty years of students, invisible, rows and rows. Wasn't that strange? She no longer remembered their names, only their faults. Tell me, how do you like teaching at Vassar?"

"I love it. And I don't believe I've ever worked harder in my life."

"And isn't it wonderful work? A teacher affects eternity; you can never tell where your influence will stop."

"Oh, I wish I could sound wise in class the way you do."

Mr. Ames chuckled.

"There's a large element of luck in teaching," he said. "So often those words of wisdom are not what you meant to say at all, and you can't even imagine why you said them. I hear you have a book of poems coming out soon."

"Not till next fall. I'll send you a copy."

Another silence.

Mr. Ames broke it. "I regret that I shall not live long enough to finish all the books I want to read. Perhaps there will be a library in heaven where I can catch up. A room with a window seat and cushions and hot chocolate. Blake says dying is like walking from one room into another. I want to go on learning. I hope there are good teachers in heaven."

A month later he was dead. My mother sent me the obituary. There was no memorial service and no good cause to which I could send the money I would have spent on flowers.

We are led out of Plato's cave through a series of disillusionments. The strong light of reason puts even our own shadows to flight. But at night, when our lives return to us in dreams, who gives a hang about reason? Suddenly, night after night, I was a student again. In my dream, I couldn't finish my Blake paper on time, and I was trying to telephone Mr. Ames at his office. The phone rang and rang and rang, till at last I heard a click and Mr. Ames's voice saying to no one in particular: "I cannot come to the phone now. Please leave a message. Do not start your message till you hear the tone."

The tone never came.

The English department has installed this devilish device, I thought. In the empty silence that followed, I left a message for him to call.

Every night I wondered why he didn't return my call, and every morning I woke up knowing.

A year after his death I received a letter from Madeline, asking if I would help her put together a book on her husband's teaching. She'd written to dozens of his former students, asking them what they remembered most about his classes.

From a letter by Rachel Beth Ryan:

What has stayed with me is not what Dr. Ames taught me about success but what he taught me about failure. I still have the comment he wrote on one of my worst stories: "This isn't your best work. But don't worry. Sometimes you have to write the piece wrong before you can get it right. You're clearing space, making room for it, just as you would for a long-awaited guest."

My biggest problem was structuring my stories. I'd see the scenes in my head but halfway into the writing I'd lose the sense of how everything fit together. I tried making outlines, but the stories only got duller and duller. Dr. Ames urged me to write the scenes I wanted to write, regardless of their order in the narrative. When he found out I was addicted to playing bridge he said, "The next time a scene occurs to you, write out a brief summary on a three-by-five card. When you've got—shall we say, a full deck?—sit down and arrange them. If you're lucky, the story will find you, and it may be a far better story than the one you set out to write. Don't use an outline. Wait for the story to show you where it wants to go. Remember, the story is the master, the writer is the servant."

Dr. Ames had great faith in the healing power of literature. The right author taken at the right time, he felt, could set a bewildered writer back on course. Sometimes I almost felt he was giving me a prescription. "Your metaphors are tired. Two ounces of Neruda and one of Emily Dickinson, to be taken at bedtime. Any book you love can be your teacher," he said, "if you read it as a writer. Study it paragraph by paragraph, sentence by sentence, word by word."

From a letter by Jay Cohen:

It shames me to remember my class with Ames. He must have found me insufferable. I was a sophomore, and I had this big crush on Alexander Pope. I wanted to be T. S. Eliot and spoke with what I hoped was an English accent. I even bought a Parker 51, though I lose pens at the rate of one a week. Unfortunately I loved all the trappings of being a writer and none of the work. Ames kept a box in his office that held fifteen slots, and above them he had written the names of his writing students. Every Friday he expected us to leave our papers in the designated slot. One day I left a note saying my poem was in progress. To my surprise, he called me in and said, "If something is in progress, you can mark it Don't Read, but you must hand it in."

I was dumbfounded. "What's the point of handing it in if you're not going to read it?"

"The point is, you will let go of it. And then the teacher in yourself can speak."

He used to say, "I'm trying to make myself obsolete." Months passed before I could acknowledge that letting go is not giving up but a way of getting distance on the poem or story, of seeing how to work on it.

Something else he taught me. There are two kinds of beginnings in fiction: the sentence that gets you started and the true opening sentence, which may not find you till you are well into the work. Ames loathed outlines. Especially in poetry, he believed logic was a terrible impediment to good writing, and he worked hard to make me forget what I'd been taught in freshman English: topic sentence, examples, conclusion. He'd cut up my poems in class and rearrange the stanzas, sometimes even the lines. Then we'd discuss other possible arrangements, and I'd leave class with all these tiny slips of paper crushed into my back pocket, looking as if I'd just run amok over a box of fortune cookies.

From a letter by William Klonsky:

Nothing that Ames told me when I was in his class helped me as much as a letter he wrote me three years ago. I was writing my third unpublished novel. And one day I took a look at the hundred or so pages I'd been grinding out for the last five months, and I realized they were no good. It wasn't just a question of revision. The whole thing was wrong: story, characters, everything. Why had it taken me so long to realize this?

At that point I decided to give up writing. And I wrote a long letter to Ames explaining why, because I felt he was the one person besides myself who would care.

Within the week he answered my letter.

Dear Bill,

You have mistaken the failure of one writing project for the total failure of yourself as a writer. Try to separate them. Put the novel aside and write something completely different. Nonfiction, perhaps. If you still feel blocked, write

me a letter describing a story you'd like to write. Make it a
very detailed letter. Trust me. Somewhere along the way,
the letter will turn into the story itself.

From a letter by John Petty:

When I signed up for "The Art of Writing," I thought I was
joining a workshop. We'd read one another's work in class and discuss
it. That's the kind of writing class I'd taken before. I'd have time to
write, and I'd write what I pleased. It was a great shock to discover
that Ames gave assignments.

"The point of assignments," he said, "is to take your imagination
to a new place. Some of you may find yourselves going back to these
exercises long after you've left this class."

He liked the word *exercises,* because it reminded him of the study
of music. I had no trouble with the fiction assignments, but the poetry
assignments were maddening. Write a poem without adjectives. Write
a poem developed from a first line. Write a poem of which the first
and third stanzas are provided. Write a dialogue in verse. Write a
revision of somebody else's bad poem. There were other assignments,
but I've forgotten them. Later I found Ames had borrowed them from
Roethke's essay "The Teaching Poet."

Of all his assignments, the one I liked best was what he called
"writing in the instructional mode." He told us that his passion for
odd instructions began when he was traveling to the Canary Islands
on a Spanish ship and found the following notice posted over a life
jacket on his cabin door: "Helpsavering Aparata. In emergings behold
many whistles! Associate the stringing apparata about the bosoms and
meet behind. Flee then to the indifferent lifesaveringshippen obedi-
encing the instructs of the vessel!"

Ames was charmed. He saw great possibilities for poetry. He asked everyone in the class to write a poem in which we instructed somebody to do something. To help us get started, he brought to class a small hand mill, the kind used for grinding coffee.

"This mill has a venerable history," he said. "It is first cousin to the mill in the fairy tale that ground an avalanche of porridge because its owner couldn't remember the words to make it stop. And it is second cousin to the mill that sits at the bottom of the sea, grinding salt till the Last Judgment. Now, write me instructions for using this mill."

There was nothing obviously magical about Ames's coffee mill. But aren't all objects magical if you consider them in the right light? Spinning wheels, brooms, rings—in fairy tales they show us their dark sides.

Whatever I wrote has gone into the great wastebasket in the sky. But I do remember what one student wrote, because it was mimeographed for class and I liked it well enough to save it:

> This mill is good for just about everything except there are a few things you must take note of.
>
> 1) Always turn the crank counterclockwise, for it produces always against the motion of the earth and time—the product is a result of friction against time.
>
> 2) Never turn it clockwise—for to do so is to compete with the stars, the moon, the sun, the earth, and all of their generative forces. They will become jealous and you will disappear, never to have been born.
>
> 3) Because of the above, never let anyone else use it, touch, see it, or even know of its existence for this could prove fatal. This is not like those natural treasures which lack all traces of human horror.[3]

The advantage of an instructional poem is its focus. You have your subject and you have your audience. Stephen Sondheim, whose songs I love, put it this way: "If you told me to write a love song tonight I'd have a lot of trouble. But if you tell me to write a love song about a girl with a red dress who goes into a bar and is on her fifth martini and is falling off her chair, that's a lot easier, and it makes me free to say anything I want."

Take the poem by William Carlos Williams that starts out, "I will teach you, my townspeople, how to perform a funeral." I knew it by heart once and still remember the ending:

> A rough plain hearse then
> with gilt wheels and no top at all.
> On this the coffin lies
> by its own weight.
>
>   No wreaths please—
> especially no hot house flowers.
> Some common memento is better,
> something he prized and is known by:
> his old clothes—a few books perhaps—
> God knows what!
>
> . . . . . .
>
> Then briefly as to yourselves:
> Walk behind—as they do in France,
> seventh class, or if you ride
> Hell take curtains! Go with some show
> of inconvenience; sit openly—
> to the weather as to grief.

Or do you think you can shut grief in?
What—from us? We who have perhaps
nothing to lose? Share with us
share with us—it will be money
in your pockets.

Go now

I think you are ready.[4]

From a letter by Jane Stewart Briggs:

In Dr. Ames's class I was writing fiction. I loved revising and reworking my stories. But I hated to end them, and one day in class I asked, "How do you know when a story is finished?" I shall never forget his answer. "There's this difference between the great artist and the Sunday painter: the great artist knows when to stop. It's almost like baking bread; you can smell when it's done, the work itself tells you."

Endings, endings. Stephen Vincent Benét wrote, "When I was in school, I knew poetry was not a dead thing. I knew it was always written by the living, even though the dateline said the man was dead."

You there, Mr. Ames, six feet under a stone in Forest Hills and sleeping in the back row, far from the gaze of the angel who presides over the graves like a teacher—and what a quiet class!—you there, she's calling on you to recite, to tell the truth. Mr. Ames, what have you to say for yourself?

We think by feeling. What is there to know?
I hear my being dance from ear to ear.
I wake to sleep, and take my waking slow.

Of those so close beside me, which are you?
God bless the Ground! I have walked softly there,
And learn by going where I have to go.

Light takes the Tree; but who can tell us how?
The lowly worm climbs up a winding stair;
I wake to sleep, and take my waking slow.

. . . .

This shaking keeps me steady. I should know.
What falls away is always. And is near.
I wake to sleep, and take my waking slow.
I learn by going where I have to go.

NOTES

[1] *The Dialogues of Plato,* Vol. I, B. Gowett, trans. (New York: Random House, 1937), 779.

[2] Theodore Roethke, "The Waking," in *The Collected Poems of Theodore Roethke* (Bantam Doubleday Dell Publishing Group, Inc., Anchor Books Edition, 1975), 104.

[3] This piece was written by Will Ostrow.

[4] William Carlos Williams, "Tract," in *The Collected Earlier Poems of William Carlos Williams* (New York: New Directions Publishing Corp., 1951), 130–31.

• • • • • • • • •

Tell all the Truth but tell it slant—
Success in Circuit lies
Too bright for our infirm Delight
The Truth's superb surprise
As Lightning to the Children eased
With explanation kind
The Truth must dazzle gradually
Or every man be blind—[1]

—Emily Dickinson

When I was growing up in Ann Arbor, Michigan, our house was known, in certain circles, for a modest enclosure on the third floor that my father called the spare room, my mother called the maid's room, my sister called the third-floor room, and I called the attic. It had a window, a closet, and a private bath. The bathtub had legs, and during vacations my mother hid the family silver in the dark space under its porcelain belly. From time to time, friends, relatives, and strangers used the room, but only as a resting place, never as a destination.

The biggest house in the neighborhood was not ours, however. No, the Zeta Beta Tau fraternity house at the end of the block was ten times larger. Spring and fall, their front yard was filled with young men playing touch football. The ZBTs, as they called themselves, had the highest grade-point average of any group on campus. This caused my mother to look favorably upon them.

One afternoon two weeks into the fall semester there came a knock at the door, and I opened it and found two young men—one blond, one dark haired—standing on the front steps. They were not Mormons; they did not wear little signs on their lapels saying Elder Smith or Elder Canfield. They were not Jehovah's Witnesses; they were not holding thin copies of the *Watchtower*.

"Hi," said the blond one. "I'm Danny Weinstein and this is Scott Greene. We're looking for a room to rent."

I was ten years old and astonished that anyone should state his business to me, as if I were a grown-up. My mother came to the door, and Danny came to the point. They were two Zeta Beta Tau pledges, he explained. The fraternity had accepted more new members than the chapter house could hold, and they needed a room in the neighborhood till space opened up for them. They'd heard about our spare room from one of the busboys. Naturally they would be taking their meals at the chapter house. After some discussion, Mother announced her decision.

"Okay," she said. "The room is yours."

Scott remained a shadowy presence in our lives who sped off to class in the morning and to the library in the evening, and moved out after six weeks. Danny stayed for the whole semester. The only book I ever saw him carrying was a fat volume with a blue butterfly on the cover and the words *The Artistic Personality* on the spine. Afternoons, when Danny came home from class he lingered on the stairs, eager to engage any of us in conversation. Why cats purr, why you should not keep tomatoes in the icebox, why baking soda is better for you than toothpaste—no matter what topic you brought up, Danny could hold forth on it, and I assumed that the fat blue book was the source of his knowledge. Because I never saw him actually reading it, I supposed he acquired his wisdom through a sort of laying-on of hands, his hands on the magic book, which sent its gifts to him through invisible currents. Would he lend it to me if I told him how badly I was doing in Miss Brandenberger's after-school Bible class, for which my mother had signed me up and which I attended but without enthusiasm?

"So what did you study in your Bible class today?" Danny asked one afternoon.

Usually I just shrugged and said, "Nothing much." But that day Miss Brandenberger had given us a quiz. I hadn't studied at all and had got about two-thirds of the questions wrong.

"We had a test on the parables of Jesus," I said. To avoid showing the test to him, I waved my Bible, which fell open to the ribbon marking 13 Matthew. Danny leaned closer and studied the page.

"My God," he said, "they've printed all the conversation in red."

"Just the Jesus parts," I corrected him.

He flipped back to the Old Testament. "Listen, Jesus got all his stuff from Solomon," he said. "They should have printed Solomon's words in red. Oh, I love parables. Without parables, the Torah would be a big maze."

At that moment, I couldn't imagine anyone loving parables. There was no mention of the Torah in our class workbook, and I didn't want to ask Danny what the Torah was for fear of complicating an already difficult subject.

"I have to correct my test for Miss Brandenberger," I told him. "It'll take hours."

"Let's see it," he said.

Danny sat down on the top step, and I handed him the test and collapsed in misery two stairs below him. He studied it for several minutes before he looked down at me.

"Your teacher made up this test?" he asked.

I nodded.

"It stinks," said Danny. "What's good she marks bad, what's bad she marks good. Now here, where she asks, 'Why did Jesus tell the parables?' you say, 'To teach people.' That she marks good."

"Isn't that the answer?"

"Oh, it's an answer," replied Danny, "but it's not the best answer. You want to get an 'A' in this class? Let me give you a really good answer. Write it down."

My salvation handed me his ballpoint pen and the blue butterfly book for a writing board.

"Once upon a time Truth used to walk around town stark naked. Think of it—not a stitch on! People were shocked. Scandalized. They shut the door on him, they avoided him, they wouldn't risk being seen with him. One day, as Truth was wandering through town, outcast, hangdog, alone, who should he happen to meet but Parable. Parable was dressed to the nines. A tuxedo, a cape, a top hat.

" 'Truth, old friend,' said Parable. 'What's the problem?'

"Truth shook his head.

" 'I'm old and ugly, brother. Nobody loves me.'

" 'Nonsense!' exclaimed Parable. 'I'm no younger than you are. Listen, brother, you've got to dress better. People don't like you going around all naked. I'll give you some of my clothes, and you'll be the life of the party.'

"Truth put on a white linen suit, a pink shirt, and a black tie, and what do you know? People invited him here, they invited him there, they shook his hand when they met him in the street. Since that time

Truth and Parable have been great friends. Everybody admires them. Even," he added, "Miss Brandenberger."[2]

I wrote down Danny's story and attached it to my quiz before handing it in. A week later it came back with a comment from Miss Brandenberger. "Interesting story. But your first answer was correct."

After Danny Weinstein moved out of our lives, my mother found the blue book on the top shelf of the closet in our spare room and gave it to me. All semester I had misread the title. The blue book with the butterfly on the cover was called *The Autistic Personality,* and it was full of charts, graphs, and psychological jargon. But I like to think that the other book, the magic one, exists somewhere, that maybe Danny took it with him and that one day he will lose the book, leave it in the Greyhound bus depot perhaps, where an old man will pick it up and, failing to recognize its true worth, will sell it to a used-book dealer, and after passing through many hands, it will fall into mine, and when I turn to the chapter on parables, I will find both what Danny said and what he might have said.

Danny Weinstein, wherever you are, these parables from *The Artistic Personality* are for you.

THE MANUSCRIPT AND THE MICROWAVE

There was once a bear who bought a great many books and so had a reputation for being extremely well read. Nobody knew that he had never finished reading a book in his life and that his true passion did not incline to literature at all but to mail-order catalogs. Evenings, he pored over their seductive promises. Beauty, strength, speed—they promised everything. There were machines to take dust from the air, answer your telephone, kill noxious insects, shrink your hips, and enlarge your biceps—all at the flick of a switch. There were books to entertain you and videos to instruct you.

One night while he was browsing through a Barnes & Noble catalog of best-selling novels, the bear said to himself, I could write one of those.

In three months he'd finished the first draft of a novel about a fox who wins a million dollars in the lottery and is hit by a car on his way to collect the money. The bear sent his novel to a wolverine he'd once dated in college who now worked for a publisher. He could hardly believe his luck when she called him into her office to discuss it.

"Your manuscript is too thin to be a novel," she said. "You need to flesh it out. It reads like a proposal. The prose is clear and sinewy, but you need more scenes, more dialogue."

Depressed, the bear left her office, hurried past the receptionist, and pushed the button for the elevator. He scarcely noticed a fox with a tattered briefcase under his paw.

"You look like a bear whose manuscript has been rejected," said the fox. "Am I right?"

The bear nodded, too upset to speak.

"So what did they tell you?" asked the fox.

"I need to flesh the story out. It's too thin to be a novel."

"Um," said the fox.

"When I think of all the work it'll take to fix it, I feel sick," said the bear.

"Time is money," said the fox. "I have the very thing to help you."

And he whipped out a colorful brochure.

The bear read: "Is your book too scrawny? Just pop it into our manuscript microwave."

"Manuscript microwave?" exclaimed the bear.

"You set it for the number of chapters you want and turn it on. It's only five hundred dollars. I happen to have an order form right here."

The bear hesitated.

"If you order now, you'll also receive our Cuisinart Word Chopper."

"I don't need a word chopper," said the bear.

"Not now, maybe," said the fox, "but who knows what the future holds?"

The bear read the order form very carefully before he filled it out. Then he wrote a check for five hundred dollars and handed it to the fox.

"When will this thing arrive?" he asked.

"In a week," said the fox. "It has to be shipped from California."

The bear stopped all work on his manuscript and spent his days mooning about the mailbox. On the seventh day, he spied a UPS truck in the driveway and rushed out to meet it.

"Sign here," said the driver.

The box was large but very light, and the bear carried it into the living room, opened it, and lifted out two parcels—one large, one small—packed in excelsior that appeared to be the shredded pages of novels. When he unwrapped the larger parcel, he could scarcely contain his delight. The manuscript microwave looked almost as simple as his old Brownie camera. All you had to do was figure out how many chapters you wanted and set the number. A button labeled Add Pages made the chapters longer or shorter. The bear opened the door of the microwave, laid his manuscript on the glass plate inside, shut the door, and set the dial for twelve.

The machine hummed pensively. Through the little window the

bear watched his manuscript puffing up like soufflé. So my novel is too thin, eh? he growled to himself. So it needs to be fleshed out, does it?

He pushed Add Pages and watched the countdown wink past on the digital timer till the bell rang. With trembling paws he took his novel out and read the first page.

Oh, where were his sinewy sentences? Somewhere under the folds of that verbose, flowery prose lay his story. Then he understood the reason for the Cuisinart Word Chopper. He pulled the Word Chopper out of its wrappings, plugged it in, dropped his novel into the plastic canister—it barely fit—and flicked the switch.

This time when he fished out his manuscript the sentences were so choppy he couldn't recognize them.

Three years later the bear published a mystery novel about a microwave salesman who wins the lottery and becomes one of the most-wanted crooks of all time.

Moral: Behind every published novel are at least two unpublishable ones. There are no shortcuts.

DIAMONDS FOR SUPPER

An attractive young magpie was standing in her kitchen, wondering what to cook for dinner. She had been married only three months and had run through the small repertoire of dishes she knew. Though her husband hadn't complained, the magpie worried about the longterm effects of ninety successive dinners of franks and beans.

She put a pot of water on the stove, hoping a cup of instant coffee would clear her brain, when suddenly the diamond in her engagement ring dropped out and sparkled its way to the bottom of the pot.

"Diamond soup!" she exclaimed. "I'll make diamond soup."

Naturally there was no recipe for diamond soup in *The Joy of Cooking,* but the magpie thought back to soups she had enjoyed in the past and counted on instinct and memory to instruct her. She thought of garnets and added carrots, she thought of pearls and added onions, she thought of jet and added peppercorns. She longed for emeralds and rubies and added rosemary and tomatoes. Amethysts crossed her mind, and she added purple sage.

When her husband came home, he exclaimed, "Something smells divine! I hope it's dinner."

"Sit down," said the magpie modestly, "and I'll serve the soup."

As she was about to ladle it into two bowls, the diamond called to her, "Take me out."

"But you're brilliant," said the magpie. "You're beautiful."

"This soup by any other name would taste as good," said the diamond. "Take me out. Do you want your husband to break a tooth?"

Moral: The line you love best is the hardest to cut.

A Feast for the Ears

There was once a young parrot who longed to become a chef.

"Okay," said his father, "you can apprentice yourself to a master chef, or you can go to cooking school."

The parrot enrolled at the Culinary Institute of Birds. Right away everyone could see he would go far. For "Introduction to Feasts 101: A History of Banquets from 1000 A.D. to the Present," he handed in a paper on soup in the Middle Ages that his professor felt was publishable, and she encouraged the parrot to major in feasts, since he showed such a talent for it.

His senior year, in lieu of a thesis, the parrot chose to prepare a banquet for twelve distinguished ravens who were among the most renowned chefs in the country. On the appointed day, the ravens arrived and seated themselves at a table set with the finest china and crystal. The parrot stepped forward and made a little bow.

"I have prepared a feast that I believe will prove unlike any you have ever tasted. The only ingredients I have allowed myself are flowers."

He said he hoped the ravens would enjoy his daylily soup. He told them he'd risen before sunrise to gather the daylilies and he'd cooked them in a fine French sherry.

"Some people," he added, "cook the buds. But I use only the blossoms. And these daylilies are not the common variety."

He told them of a clearing in the middle of a forest to the east where the finest lilies grew. He told them it took five hours to reach the place by car and another hour on foot, since neither roads nor trails disturbed the forest.

"Some people wouldn't go to so much trouble," he said. "But you have only to compare the wild lily with the garden variety to taste the difference."

A raven at the head of the table raised his wing. "It sounds wonderful. We're all famished. Where is the food?"

"I . . . I haven't started cooking it yet," stammered the parrot, "but wait till you hear my menu."

Moral: If you start your story with a clutter of details, you'll never get to the main course.

THE RIVER AND THE MAP

On the edge of a vast forest lived two coyotes who made their living chopping wood. All day the brothers sawed and chopped and hauled wood, and in the evening they sat around with their coyote buddies in the Racoon Saloon and talked about what lay on the other side of the forest.

"Fame and fortune," said the bartender. "That's why nobody ever comes back."

One night the younger brother turned to the older brother and said, "Let's cross the forest. What have we got to lose?"

"Our lives," said the older brother.

"The world is a strange place," said the younger brother, "and nobody gets out of it alive. If you won't come with me, I'll go alone."

The older brother wouldn't hear of that, so he asked this animal and that animal for help, and at last he found a beaver who offered to sell him a map for five cords of maple chopped small. The map showed a path winding through the forest. In the right-hand bottom corner were the numbers 1801.

"It's a little out of date," said the beaver. "If it doesn't work as a map, you can use it as a decorative item for your den."

The next morning the brothers set out, and they were delighted to find a path that ran beside the river just as the map promised. Toward evening, however, the path forked, with the left-hand fork leading away from the river.

"According to the map," said the older brother, "we should go to the left."

"That doesn't feel right," said the younger brother. "I'm for following the river. A river has a beginning, a middle, and an end. The path could lead to nothing."

"Not this path," said the older brother. "It's on the map."

"You follow the map, and I'll follow the river," said the younger brother, "and let's see who arrives first."

They hugged each other good-bye. The older brother set off clutching the map in his paw and was never seen again. The younger brother had his own troubles. The forest grew so dense he could not even see the river. But he could hear it—sometimes close, sometimes distant—and after a long, difficult journey he stepped out into a glorious garden on the other side.

Moral: Though you may be lost, your story is not. It is waiting for you to catch up with it.

THE WINGLESS VAMPIRE BAT OF GREATER BROOKLYN

A cat saw a mouse emerging from the local movie theater, and since the cat had not eaten for two days, he pounced, bit the mouse in the neck, and was about to finish him off when he noticed a policeman and a cockroach hurrying toward them.

"You're under arrest!" shouted the policeman.

"It's the mouse you should arrest, not me," said the cat. "He's number one on the most-wanted list of bloodsucking animals."

The policeman turned to the mouse. "What do you have to say for yourself?"

In a trembling voice, the mouse replied, "Officer, I was on my way home from the movies when the cat jumped me. He gave me a nasty gash in my neck. I yanked his whiskers and pulled out two of them, but that didn't stop him. If this cockroach hadn't come along, I'd be a kitty hors d'oeuvre."

"That's right," said the cockroach. "The cat jumped the mouse and bit him in the neck."

With the back of his paw, the cat was wiping mouse blood from his lips. The policeman read the cat his rights.

"Anything you say can be used against you," said the policeman. "Now, what happened?"

The cat closed his eyes. "Officer, three years ago I was kidnapped by the Wingless Vampire Bat of Greater Brooklyn. If not for some quick work on the part of Sergeant O'Leary, who happened to be on duty that night, the bat would have killed me. Do you know Sergeant O'Leary?"

"No," said the policeman.

"A pity. Well, unlike other bats, the Wingless Vampire Bat, as you know, not only swoops, he can run. Three years ago to the day I was walking home from the movies and the bat grabbed me. The last thing I saw before I passed out was his hideous shadow darkening the wall around the corner from the theater."

The cat paused and wiped his eyes.

"Pardon me," he said. "These recollections are still painful, even after three years of therapy with Doctor Calzone. Do you know Doctor Calzone?"

"No," said the policeman.

"Too bad. He could tell you how severely the experience affected me. And tonight as I was on my way to the movies, I caught sight of the shadow of the Wingless Vampire Bat high over the marquee. The bat swooped. I was so terrified I shed two of my whiskers. I made a rush at the shadow and bit down hard."

"Wait a minute," said the policeman. "The cockroach says you attacked the mouse."

The cat cast a sneering glance at the cockroach. "Officer, how could this cockroach have possibly seen anything? Nothing is darker than the Vampire Bat's shadow."

"You have mouse blood on your mouth," said the cockroach.

"That's not mouse blood," said the cat. "My gums are in such bad shape they bleed at the slightest touch. Officer, arrest this mouse.

He is the Wingless Vampire Bat of Greater Brooklyn—a monster of deception and lies. I barely escaped with my life."

"You've got to believe me, Officer," squeaked the mouse. "I'm telling you the truth. I'm telling you what really happened."

The policeman arrested the mouse.

Moral: Not whether it happened but whether the reader believes it happened—that's what counts.

THE SEASHELL IN THE DESERT

A pilot widely known for his skill as a navigator was flying his plane across the desert at the edge of the Indian Ocean. Suddenly the engine sputtered and died, and he had to make an emergency landing. The pilot was very calm. He knew that if he managed his supplies carefully he had enough water and food on board to last him for a month, and he was sure another traveler would find him before the month was out.

He consulted his atlas of the region, which contained a detailed map.

"The sun is due east; the water was on my left when I entered this area, though I can't see it now. It is logical to conclude I am in the region called the Desert of Despair."

He noticed what appeared to be a pile of stones on the horizon, and after sundown, when the air was cooler, he walked over to investigate and was astonished to discover the ruins of a city. From the center of the ruins rose a tower.

"Obviously a fortress," he said to himself. "But against whom?"

At that moment something winked at him from the sand, and glancing down, he spied six small but winsome conch shells fastened together by dried seaweed like a present. Light sparkled on the iridescent lip of each one so seductively that the pilot had to fight a primitive urge to pick them up and hang them around his neck.

Now here was a mystery. Conchs do not thrive in the desert.

"It is logical to conclude that the sea must have covered this place recently," said the pilot to himself, "since the seaweed is not yet brittle and the conch makes its home in deep waters."

Then he reflected that tropical waters bring tropical storms and tidal waves that rush far inland and destroy entire villages.

"Only a crazy man would spend another night on the ground. And I'm not crazy. I'll do the right thing. I shall move into the top room of the tower. When the tidal wave comes, it will not find me."

The pilot set to work hauling his supplies up the forty-four steps of the tower. The room at the top was small—just big enough for one or two people standing close together to gaze up at the sky.

"Perhaps the king of this place built it to save himself and his family," said the pilot, who, lacking other company, had started talking to himself.

He'd taken to sleeping with his binoculars around his neck, and he looked through them often. The tidal wave would not catch him napping—no indeed. During the day he read his atlas and exercised by walking up and down the forty-four steps and considering the actions he might have taken if he hadn't found the seashells.

"I've done the sensible thing," he told himself.

His supplies of food and water were almost gone, and still the sun rose and set and no travelers passed that way.

On the last day of the month the man stood on his tower and

lifted his binoculars and saw, galloping toward him, three camels loaded with supplies.

"Hallo!" he called. "Hallo!"

But at such a distance and with the wind blowing, who could hear him? No use, he told himself, to run down the forty-four steps and flag them down. The camels would be gone by the time he reached the bottom.

"Hallo!"

Through his binoculars they appeared so close that he could see the faces of the drivers and the bridles of the beasts, decorated with small but winsome conch shells fastened to the leather with strands of seaweed. And as the pilot stared, a seashell dropped off the bridle of the first camel and remained like an iridescent wink on the empty face of the sand.

Moral: Take risks. It is safer to be crazy than dull.

THE ARTIST AND THE GOAT

Lord Derby prided himself on the variety of exotic beasts he kept in a private zoo he maintained on his estate in the south of England. He owned panthers and peacocks, zebras, fallow deer, and Barbary apes. Of all his acquisitions, none pleased him more than a rare mountain goat that had been sent to him by a veterinarian from Colorado. She was the only goat scientists had ever seen who carried a thread of gold and three freshwater pearls twisted into her tiny black horns.

The goat was very shy and seldom showed herself.

"Why don't you have her portrait painted?" suggested Lady Derby. "On the days she doesn't come around, we can look at her picture."

Lord Derby thought this an excellent idea. He advertised in the newspaper for an artist to paint the portrait of his Colorado mountain goat and added that if the work was satisfactory he would commission the artist to do a portrait of himself and Lady Derby as well.

The newspaper had scarcely hit the stands when an artist knocked at the Derby mansion and presented himself for the job.

"Are you familiar with the mountain goats of Colorado?" asked Lord Derby.

"Don't worry," replied the artist. "I was born in Colorado."

Because the artist was hungry, he did not say that he was born in a small town called Colorado (population three hundred) located in northeast Iowa and that he had never seen a mountain in his life. Lord Derby hired him on the spot, and Lady Derby showed him his room and his studio, gave him a tour of the grounds, and pointed out the mountain goat's favorite haunts.

The artist started work that very day. But the mountain goat of Colorado was more elusive than he'd ever dreamed she would be. It took him three months to make his preliminary sketches and another month to finish the picture. Eagerly he summoned Lord and Lady Derby to his studio. They stood and stared at the painting in silence.

"Well?" said the artist. "What do you think?"

"It's a goat all right," said Lord Derby, "but it's not my goat. My goat's horns are black with a stripe of gold and three freshwater pearls twisted into them."

"Your goat moved so fast I couldn't get a good look at her horns," said the artist. "But that's a small mistake. Do you want me to start work on your portrait tomorrow?"

"Certainly not," said Lord Derby. "If you let a small mistake pass into your work, how can I trust you not to make a large one?"

Moral: The grass of fiction grows on the soil of fact. A single error can infect a whole story.

THE GHOSTLY PLAYERS

Once upon a time in Detroit there was a haunted theater. People in search of free entertainment used to go there. If you were lucky, you could watch a cast of ghosts doing the plays they'd performed while they were alive. What made the experience so strange was the total indifference of the ghosts to applause. They took no notice of the living. The owner of the theater did nothing to disturb the place, which was badly in need of repair. When he died, the theater was sold to an energetic young director who had often enjoyed these ghostly performances.

"What this place needs," he said, "is some new material."

He had just finished a play based on the life of Elvis Presley. What a perfect choice for opening the new season! He cleared the stage of debris and called the ghosts to rehearsal. Shyly, from behind curtains and mirrors, down stairways and balconies, the ghosts came, to see if the new director could be trusted.

"First of all, I'm not holding auditions," he said. "I've watched all of you perform, and I'm going to assign the parts."

And he handed out copies of the script. As he moved from one to the other, it seemed to him that his actors were growing fainter. But what could you expect of ghosts?

At the first rehearsal, however, only half the ghosts showed up. At the second rehearsal, none of them showed up. No amount of threatening or coaxing could persuade them to return. The young director lost interest in the theater and put it up for sale. For two weeks no one made him an offer.

On the first day of the third week the telephone rang and a woman's voice said, "I'm interested in your theater."

"The best offer takes it," said the director.

"Are you selling it because it's haunted?" asked the woman.

"No, I'm selling it because it's *not* haunted. When I bought it, a whole cast of these wonderful characters lived there, but I haven't seen them in ages."

"I can help you," said the woman. "Meet me at the theater tomorrow."

The next morning the woman was waiting for him. He unlocked the door, switched on the lights, and showed her the empty stage.

"Tell me about the ghosts," said the woman. "Who are they?"

"Well, one of them is an old man. I think he has arthritis. He can hardly walk."

"So how do you expect him to come if he can't walk? Get a walker and leave it onstage."

"Oh, he'd never use a walker," said the director. "He's very proud. A cane, maybe, but never a walker."

"So get him a cane."

The director rummaged through the prop box and found a cane that he leaned against a chair in the middle of the stage. The woman examined it.

"Not good enough," she said.

"What's wrong with it?"

"It looks like just what the doctor ordered. Didn't you say he was proud? Find a fancy one. The old man wants people to think he's carrying it because it's beautiful and for no other reason."

The director fished through the prop box and pulled out a walking stick with the head of a greyhound carved on the handle. This he leaned against the chair instead of the cane.

"Now, about the other ghosts," said the woman.

"Well, there's a girl I think is his daughter," said the director. "She hates the old man. She says she'd like to slam the door in his face."

"How do you expect her to slam a door that doesn't exist? Get her a door."

The director found a door in the basement, dragged it upstairs, and set it up on the stage.

"How am I doing?" he asked.

"Don't ask me," whispered the woman. "Ask them."

And she pointed to the old man, who was leaning on the walking stick and taking a few tentative steps, and to the young girl, who was opening and closing the door and smiling.

Moral: Trust your characters. Their story is not your story. You are the window through which their lives pass.

THE BUZZARD AND AESOP'S FABLE

A buzzard running for governor of the forest was invited one evening to speak to a large gathering of prospective voters, mostly rich owls who were known to be undecided. The polls showed the election would be a close one. The buzzard reminded them of his good political record. He'd voted to save the elms. He'd voted for zoning against termites. He supported medical benefits for all birds, and for rich owls in particular. He pointed out how the incumbent governor, a fox, favored mammals and did nothing to help other forms of life. He spoke of lower taxes, better housing for wrens, cleaner water for swans.

The night was hot, and the owls grew drowsy. At this moment Aesop strolled by. Noting the snoozing owls, he tapped the buzzard on the shoulder and said, "You'll never win the election that way."

"What else can I do?" asked the buzzard.

Aesop stood up and addressed the crowd. "Once upon a time there was a fox, a buzzard, and an owl. And one day—"

Instantly he had their complete attention.

Moral: Show, don't tell. Information touches the mind, story sinks into the heart.

THE LIONESS AND THE RIVER

The king of the beasts came down with a terrible case of lion flu. His queen, the lioness, called the court physician, who examined the lion and shook his head.

"I can do nothing more for your husband. But on the other side of the river a hundred miles to the east is a garden, and in that garden is a well and in that well runs the water of life. Run to that well as quickly as you can and bring back a cup of the water of life."

"I'll send my swiftest runner," said the lioness.

"No," said the doctor. "You must fetch it yourself, my dear. No one else can save the king."

The lioness was an excellent runner, but she was also the queen, and she was accustomed to traveling in style. She ordered a dozen servants to pack provisions for the journey and four hyenas to fetch her sedan chair. She put on her richest gown of hyssop green, trimmed with bear claws, which are known to protect the wearer from all danger. Last of all her lioness-in-waiting set the golden crown on her head, adjusting it carefully between the queen's ears.

The party set out through the forest, and in two days they reached the river. Peeking out from her sedan chair, the queen spied the garden on the opposite side. Suddenly the hyenas set her chair down on the riverbank.

"This is no time to stop!" shouted the lioness.

"Your Highness," said a young hyena, "there's no bridge and the current is very swift."

"No bridge?" exclaimed the lioness. "How do animals cross?"

"I see a rope laid over the water," said the hyena. "You could walk on that."

The lioness climbed down, took off her clothes, and clutching the rope between her paws she teetered and tipped her way across while the hyenas roared with laughter.

"Your crown!" called the lady-in-waiting. "You forgot your crown."

"I'll travel in style later," called the lioness. "Right now all I want to do is cross the water."

Moral: The explorer doesn't stop because the road is not perfect. Don't be afraid to write badly.

THE NATURALIST AND THE ZIGELOT

There once was a naturalist who drank too much wine at his birthday party, and late in the evening he boasted to a friend, "I can tame any animal. Any animal at all."

"A lion?" asked the friend.

The naturalist snorted. "I've had lions eating out of my hand."

"A grizzly bear?" asked the friend. "You've tamed grizzly bears?"

"I never met a bear I didn't like. The secret is talking to them in their own language."

The friend smiled. "How about the great American zigelot?"

That stumped the naturalist, who had never even heard of the great American zigelot. But of course he did not want to admit it.

"Don't believe I've ever seen one," said the naturalist.

"There are zigelot tracks under the locust tree behind your house," said the friend, "so I thought you might have seen one. When they spread their wings, the whole forest lights up. A pity they're so hard to tame. They never come when they're called. They come when they're not called. But if a great American zigelot builds its nest near your house, you'll have good luck beyond your wildest dreams."

The next day the naturalist went to the library and read all the books and articles he could find on the care and feeding of the great American zigelot. One book said it liked silence. Another said it liked rap music. A third said it was nocturnal. A fourth said it went to bed every night at ten o'clock. All agreed on one thing, however. The zigelot was especially fond of pudding, the chief ingredient of which was yellow legal pads crushed to a powder the consistency of meal and mixed with human sweat.

The naturalist prepared a large bowl of this pudding, spooned it into seven small dishes, and put six of them in the freezer. He took a dish of pudding to the garden and sat down in the living room by his picture window to wait. No zigelot appeared. The only animal to visit him that day was a crow that pecked around the edge of the dish but did not touch the pudding.

During the night, however, the pudding disappeared. The naturalist opened his freezer and took out a frozen pudding and discovered it had turned to an unsavory pulp. "Some things have to be served fresh or not at all," he muttered, and he threw out the whole mess.

A week later his friend called to ask if he'd tamed the zigelot yet.

"No," said the naturalist, "but I think it's eating my food."

"You made the pudding again?"

"I'm up at seven o'clock working on it every day," replied the naturalist.

After two weeks all the naturalist had to show for his efforts was a very friendly crow.

"I know, I know," said the crow. "You're like everybody else. They're all waiting for the zigelot. My advice is, while you're waiting for the zigelot, settle for the crow."

That seemed like good advice. Still, the naturalist hesitated.

"The watched zigelot never flies," cautioned the crow.

So the naturalist stopped watching. He still put out the dish of fresh pudding every morning, but he put out a little treat for the crow as well. The crow visited every day and taught him the language and history of crows, and the naturalist taught the crow the language and history of humans, and they were so encouraged by each other's progress that they decided to have a party.

"I'll bring stuffed mushrooms," said the naturalist, and with his mind on nothing but mushrooms he set off to pick the puffballs he'd seen growing under the locust tree.

"Wait," said the crow. "Shall we invite the zigelot?"

"The zigelot can come when it damn well pleases."

Suddenly the whole forest lit up. Peering into the branches overhead, the naturalist spied a magnificent bird with golden wings settling down on her nest.

TWO SISTERS AND A HOUSE

Two sisters were invited to an open house given by a friend of their deceased father. Neither of them could recall ever having met the friend, but both remembered what their father had said about him: "He's traveled all over the world. You can't imagine the adventures he's had. And his house is absolutely fascinating. He designed it himself. It's like a museum full of marvels."

Naturally the sisters could hardly wait to meet the gentleman and see these marvels. On the evening of the party the younger woman was so slow in getting dressed that the older one said, "I'll go on ahead and meet you there. I don't want to miss a single moment."

And she called a cab and gave the driver the address. When they arrived, he asked her which door she wanted.

"The front door," replied the woman.

"And which door is that?" asked the driver.

Well might he ask. There were at least twenty-five doors by which the house could be entered. The driver cruised up and down the street while the woman examined them all. She finally chose the door closest to the center. It had columns and steps leading to a little round porch and looked more imposing than the others. She paid the driver and marched up the steps. When she rang the bell, the door opened and the woman was dismayed to find herself alone in a large living room. All the furnishings were beige—from the carpet to the nubby wing chairs hidden under shiny plastic covers. The room looked like the lobby of a third-class motel—everything tasteful, everything dull. It was impossible to imagine interesting people living here.

The woman wandered into several adjacent rooms but met no one.

"I must have the wrong time," she said to the air, "and I certainly have the wrong place." She was relieved to find a telephone on the coffee table, and she called for the cab to take her home.

When she got back, her younger sister was gone. The woman clicked on the TV. Only the Weather Channel came through clearly, and she watched till she fell asleep.

She was awakened by her younger sister coming in at two A.M., breathless with excitement.

"Where were you?" she exclaimed. "I've never met so many remarkable people. And you should have seen the house! The living room had a sycamore tree growing right through the roof. In the crown of the tree there was an aviary with hundreds of birds. You never heard such exquisite singing in all your life."

"What are you talking about?" said the older sister. "The living room was nothing but beige junk."

"You went in through the front door," said the younger girl. "When I saw that beige room, I figured the real entrance must be somewhere else. So I kept trying different doors until I found the right one."

Moral: Look for your real beginning a couple of pages into your rough draft.

THE PLEASURE DOME

A camel who sold books for a large textbook company was transferred from Cleveland to Fairbanks, Alaska. His first week in town, he called the Beaver Real Estate Company and said he wanted to buy a house.

"New house? Old house?" asked the pleasant-voiced beaver at the other end of the phone.

"I don't know," said the camel. "Something with charm."

"I have the very place for you," said the beaver. "Meet me at the corner of Madge and Market."

On one side of the street stood a new house, spacious and full of light. The beaver, however, led him to a Victorian mansion on the other side.

"It needs a bit of work," said the beaver. "Nobody has lived in it for two years. But wait till you see the interior."

No sooner had the camel stepped inside the house than he fell in love with it.

"I'll take it," he said. "Where do I sign?"

He called his wife and told her the good news. "I've found the house of our dreams," he assured her. "You'll love it."

His boss warned him: "Don't buy that house. There are bear tracks in the basement and bees in the attic. The rooms are small and dark. The furnace is a hundred years old. And there's no insulation."

But what did the camel care? The house on which he had set his heart had a painted cupola in the dining room. When you looked up, you saw angels bursting through rosy clouds. For the sake of those angels, the camel and his wife bought the house and moved in at once.

Almost as if the house had been waiting for this moment, it began to show them its worst side. The furnace broke, the hot-water heater exploded, the kitchen plaster dropped, and a pipe in the bathroom sent water pouring through the ceiling into the living room below. No sooner had the camel fixed the ceiling than the cupola developed a leak. The camel and his wife did not notice it until one morning a tremendous crash woke them. The cupola lay in ruins, the roof open to the sky. By the hard light of noon, the camel was surprised to see how crudely the angels were painted.

"If we lower the ceiling and put a wall between the rooms and a stairway here—," muttered the camel.

His wife was not listening. She was gazing at the new house across the street.

Moral: Complications added to a weak plot will not save it.

THE PARABLE OF THE PRODIGAL STORY

There was once a family of mice known for its hospitality to strangers. In the family burrow, which was spacious and well furnished, the mice kept one room at the back free for whomever might need it on short notice.

Now it happened that one day the youngest mouse heard a knock at the door, and when she opened it, whom should she meet but two young rooks looking for a room. The rookery had more birds than it could hold, they told her. The mouse mother heard their story and made her decision.

"The room is yours," she said, "but you have to make your own beds."

The smaller of the two rooks left after six weeks and moved back into the rookery. But the other bird stayed on. The youngest mouse liked him, because he knew so many stories. Stories are like people, he told her. They travel here and there, they go off to seek their fortunes. Of all the stories he told her, one lodged in her mind. It was a story about truth and parable. The mouse wrote it down for her teacher, who told her it was not the right answer.

So the mouse grew up and forgot the story. But stories are more patient than their listeners, and the story did not forget her. One day she heard a knock at the door, and there stood the story with a book under its arm, looking so changed she didn't recognize it till she spied a butterfly drying its azure wings under the title of the book, *The Artistic Personality*.

"Where have you been all this time?" exclaimed the mouse.

"With you," answered the story. "You've been carrying me around in your head for ages. The more you changed, the more I changed."

"Why couldn't you have come sooner?" asked the mouse.

"Why couldn't you see me?" asked the story, and opened the book to the first page for the mouse to read:

Tell all the Truth but tell it slant—
Success in Circuit lies
Too bright for our infirm Delight
The Truth's superb surprise
As Lightning to the Children eased
With explanation kind
The Truth must dazzle gradually
Or every man be blind.

NOTES

[1] Emily Dickinson, *The Poems of Emily Dickinson,* Thomas H. Johnson, ed. (Massachusetts: The Belknap Press of Harvard University Press, 1955), 792.

[2] A version of this story can be found in Nathan Ausubel's "Truth in Gay Clothes," in *A Treasury of Jewish Folklore* (New York: Crown Publishers, 1948), 13.

TRUTHS THE DEVIL TOLD ME:

POEMS AND PARABLES

•　　•　　•　　•　　•　　•　　•　　•　　•

I am going to tell you a story, and though its outside dress is false, I hope the inside is true, and of such lies may we all be guilty.

Once upon a time in Iceland, just north of Oddi, the devil ran a school. The school was famous for both its director and its alumni. All the best magicians and poets studied there—and a few holy men as well. The front door was niched into a hillside, and above the door the devil had written: You May Come In. Your Soul Is Lost.

An old crow with a chain on its left leg was the doorkeeper, and he let people in, but he never let them out; they had to manage that another way, which I will tell you presently. The school had other entrances in other hillsides all over the world, for the devil has heavy investments in real estate. But this was the first door and the oldest.

Beyond the door lay a great hall comfortably furnished with leather armchairs and oak tables and lamps that hung from chains, and the candles in the lamps gave off an invigorating fragrance of pine, and the light they threw over you was as warm and pleasant as an old shawl. The walls of the room were slate; chalk and erasers were furnished on request.

There were no schoolmasters in this school, and no administrators. Every evening the students gathered in the great hall to make their requests. You had only to whisper your question through a hole in the wall that an innocent visitor might have taken for a hot-air register, and the next morning you found a book by your chair containing precisely the information you'd asked for. If your question required a brief answer, you found it written on the walls. Ask and it shall be given to you—that was the rule here.

The residence requirement was three years, during which time the devil furnished room and board. There were gardens to walk in and entertainments and banquets, but the students never saw anyone except one another. At the end of three years the devil appeared and gave each student his final exam. To every student a different exam. A magician might be asked to raise a forest in the Sahara and candy all the trees with ice. A holy man might be told to raise the Unknown Soldier from the dead. Not so difficult if you are a capable magician. Not so difficult if you are a practicing holy man. But one impediment caused even the most brilliant students to fail, and that was the fear of failure. Whoever failed the exam was changed into a door leading from the devil's school to the world outside, each with its attendant doorkeeper, a sentient door with its memories and longings intact but without song or speech.

Does the school still exist? Belief in the devil has fallen off these days, and with it the enrollment, but if I knocked at that door hidden in the hills of Iceland, I like to think that the old crow would still come limping out to receive me.

"Student of what?" inquires the crow.

"Student of poetry," I tell him.

The crow flaps his wings twice, the air under them sighs, and he ushers me inside. *Bang!* goes the door behind me. From that hour forward I am given sonnets for breakfast, limericks for lunch, villanelles under glass for supper. I can rhyme rivers, scan the sea, count the syllables in the south wind and the accents in the pulse of a summer evening. All poets were magicians once, who by the power of their utterances raised mountains and woke the dead: "Let there be light: and there was light. Lazarus, come forth."

So I am given metaphors for my meat, rhetoric for my recreation, and at the end of three years the devil appears to give me my exam. He has neither horns nor tail. He wears a three-piece suit, a beard, and rimless glasses.

"You have accepted the conditions," he says.

"Yes," I falter.

"If you fail the test, I shall turn you into a door."

"If I fail the test, you will turn me into a door."

"Do you want a particular location? Killarney? Buenos Aires?"

"Let's just get on with the exam," I answer.

He nods and motions me to follow him. At the end of a long corridor, he turns to a blank wall, chalks an image of a curtain on it, and pushes the curtain and holds it back for me. What I see leaves me speechless. Crammed into a room that stretches to infinity on all four sides—for the wall we came through has quite disappeared—are bananas, trumpets, Cadillacs, doorknobs, whistles, fountain pens, plungers, and crowns. Nothing less than everything.

"I have one of everything in the world," says the devil. "Take a look around."

Like a buyer at the auction of some vast estate, I walk down aisles lined with mirrors, avenues built on bedsprings. But what most pleases me is a moon the size of a volleyball hanging in midair—just within my reach. Of course, it isn't a real moon. My common sense tells me the moon is too large for even a poet to hold. But my uncommon sense tells me the moon can talk; that I could light my way through the darkest woods with the moon in my hand; that the moon is a goddess; that the man who lives in the moon was placed there by the Lord (says the legend), for chopping wood on the Sabbath. A pack of lies! But if the devil's moon is false in its dimensions, it is true in my experience of it.

All my life I have longed for the moon. Now I stretch forth my hand and bring it down. It is the color of old piano keys. And it has a face, just as it does in the almanacs.

"You have chosen your exam," says the devil, smiling.

I stand there, holding the moon. "The moon is my exam?"

"Write a poem about the moon," says the devil. "You will have till the rising of the sun to finish."

"How will I know if I've passed?"

"If you pass the exam, the moon in your hand will disappear, and you will find yourself back in the world from which you came and under the real moon, which to my taste is not nearly so charming as this one. Good-bye."

Fortunately, since this is only a story, I can, if I wish, say good-bye to both the devil and the moon and step comfortably back into the world of common sense, which we like to call the real world. Because my story sounds fantastic, it may surprise you to learn that something very much like it actually did take place. In 1956, in France, a book of remarkable poems was published. They were written by an eight-year-old girl, Minou Drouet. More than fourteen thousand copies of her book sold in two weeks, but even her admirers wondered if the girl had really written the poems herself. To allay suspicions, Minou agreed to take a test for membership in the Society of Authors, Composers, and Music Publishers. She was given a list of topics, put into a room alone, and told to write a poem. The topic she chose was "Paris Sky," and the closing lines of her poem run as follows:

> I feel you so near, so heavy
> so open like a battlefield
> hairy with grass the color of blood
> that I feel—I know not why—
> my whole body resting on you
> the road has no more meaning for me
>
> . . . .
>
> my body is so welded to you, sky,
> that I am walking on my head.[1]

The poem took twenty-five minutes to write, and when the child was told she had passed the exam, she shouted, "I've won!" quite as if she'd emerged from a fight against some invisible opponent. Perhaps "I've won" is the right thing to say when you've finished a poem. The invisible opponent is whatever offers you resistance. It may also be whatever starts you off, a particular form—the sonnet, the villanelle—or a particular occasion: Dear Sir, We are compiling an anthology of poems on the American landscape. Could you send us some of your work for consideration? Dear Madam, Could you honor us with your presence and one of your poems at our Phi Beta Kappa banquet in April? Surely one of the oddest requests in the history of poetry went to Thomas Hardy when he was invited to write a book of poems suitable for the library of Queen Mary's dollhouse. The manuscript, he was informed, could not exceed three and a half inches in either the horizontal or the vertical dimension. Hardy complied. Which goes to show that a good poet can turn the most unlikely limitations to his own advantage.

If the devil gives you subjects for poetry, then surely those who teach on the side of the angels give you forms and occasions. By this criterion, Theodore Roethke is the archangel of poetry teachers. Here is his summary of the forms and occasions he gave his students:

> The scheme is that every student pursue his own bent, write the poems he wants to write—and also do at least some set exercises as a discipline. The discipline may lie in composing a poem without adjectives; a poem based on adjectives—or perhaps sets of verbs, nouns, and adjectives; a straight observational piece, with or without analogy; a poem based on a single figure; a revision of someone else's bad poem (Braithwaite and Moult are rich mines of examples); a translation; a poem developed from a first line; a poem of which first and third stanzas are provided; a song (some make a setting, too); a poem involving an

incident; a piece of original rhythmical prose—and later a poem evolved from it; a dialogue in verse; a "hate" poem; or a letter in verse.

He can embrace the form or resist it—either result can be useful.[2]

Minou Drouet, without ever having heard of Roethke, had the presence of mind to avail herself of one of his suggestions: a letter in verse—though she does not open with *Dear Sky* or close with *Sincerely yours*. Those to whom we address our best poems are not only worth noticing, they are worth loving (or hating). For a serious poet, the number of correspondents to whom he should write is staggering. Let Pablo Neruda stand as a model for us all; few men ever kept in touch with so many so faithfully. His *Odas Elementales* can be read as love letters to our oldest friends: air, salt, sadness, stars, bees, onions. Here is the opening of, and an excerpt from, his "Ode to an Onion":

> Onion,
> luminous flask,
> petal by petal
> was your beauty fashioned,
> crystalline scales your girth increased
> and, hidden in the dark earth,
> your belly swelled with dew.
> . . . . . .
> Star of the poor,
> fairy godmother,
> enveloped
> in delicate paper,

you emerge from earth
eternal, integral, a pure
celestial offshoot.
And at the chop
of the kitchen knife,
there wells up
the only tear we shed
without woe.
Without afflicting us you made us weep.[3]

Write a poem that describes something: an onion, a loaf of bread, a star. It's a favorite assignment of writing teachers, because it sounds so simple to do and is, in fact, so difficult to do well that even Ezra Pound found himself longing for a language of pictographs. When a Chinese poet writes the word *horse* and *man* or *woman* or *mouth,* says Pound, the character itself carries a picture of the thing it names. But our language works against us. It abstracts what things have in common, not what they are in particular. The onion is round. So is a basketball, a grapefruit, a globe, the moon. How does the onion's roundness differ from theirs?

Nothing less than metaphor can help us here, the apt use of which, Aristotle tells us, is "the swift perception of relations . . . the true hallmark of genius." I think that for the best poets, metaphor becomes a habit, a cast of mind. No one demonstrates this so well as Gerard Manley Hopkins, whose journals record his struggle to find the image or verb that will bring his subject into perfect focus. "I have particular periods of admiration for particular things in Nature," Hopkins remarked, "for a certain time I am astonished at the beauty of a tree." Here are three excerpts from his journal during the years 1872 and 1873:

March 26—Snow fallen upon the leaves had in the night coined or morselled itself into pyramids like hail.

August 19—I looked down from the cliffs at the sea breaking on the rocks at highwater of a spring tide . . . it is an install of green marble knotted with ragged white . . .

June 16—I looked at the pigeons down in the kitchen yard . . . The two young ones are all white and the pins of the folded wings, quill pleated over quill, are like crisp and shapely cuttleshells found on the shore. The others are dull thunder colour or black-grape-colour. . . . I saw one up on the eaves of the roof: as it moved its head a crush of satin green came and went, a wet or soft flaming of the light.[4]

There is no shock quite like that of a familiar word used in a totally unfamiliar way: the snow *morselled,* the quills *pleated,* the green wave *knotted*. A good metaphor can change your life. Nobody ever married or murdered anyone because of a metaphor. Nevertheless, before I read Neruda, I never saw onions as luminous flasks. I peeled them and wept. But that is how the onion must have looked in the Garden of Eden: beautiful and useless. There was, you remember, no hunger in Eden.

Were there metaphors in Eden? Perhaps. But the inhabitants of the garden were innocent. If there were metaphors, I suppose they were called riddles. Many an honored poet—from the writers of the Bible to Mother Goose to Emily Dickinson—has made use of the riddle form. It may be a single line, as in this Anglo-Saxon riddle that is also one of the most vivid descriptions of an icicle I know: "On the way a miracle: water became bone."[5]

When Emily Dickinson sent her nephew the gift of a cocoon, she enclosed a riddle, the answer to which was the cocoon itself.

> Drab habitation of whom?
> Tabernacle or tomb,
> Or dome of worm,
> Or porch of gnome
> Or some elf's catacomb.[6]

In the best riddles, the answer trails behind it larger questions. You will remember the riddle that the Sphinx put to Oedipus. What goes on four legs in the morning, two legs at noon, and three legs in the evening? You remember the answer: Man in infancy, maturity, and old age. If the Sphinx had really wanted to stump Oedipus, she should have told him the answer and then asked, Where is the man going?

To include riddles among the forms and occasions of serious poetry makes poetry sound like child's play, a game. Writing is a game, a holy game—the phrase is May Sarton's—and what a character in a novel by Virginia Woolf says about the way she shapes her life could also be said about the way we shape our poems: "There is a square: there is an oblong. The players take the square and place it upon the oblong. They place it very accurately; they make a perfect dwelling-place. Very little is left outside."[7]

If poetry is a game, how do we play against this invisible opponent who is really a part of ourselves? I believe the first move in the game is paying the right kind of attention to your subject, the pure, free-floating attention with which the analyst, says Freud, should listen to the patient. Randall Jarrell describes the difference between pure and applied attention in this way:

Concentration, note-taking, listening with a set—a set of pigeonholes—makes it difficult or impossible for the analyst's unconscious to respond to the patient's; takes away from the analyst the possibility of learning from the patient what the analyst doesn't already know; takes away from him all those random guesses or intuitions or inspirations which come out of nowhere—and come, too, out of the truth of the patient's being.[8]

Second, a game needs rules that free the players to move about the board. The variety of rules, which I have called forms and occasions, that writers set up for themselves is simply amazing. A student of mine who wished to purge her poetry of verbosity set herself the task of limiting her vocabulary to a list of words that a seventh-grade reader would be expected to know. But this is abundance compared to the assignment that a writing teacher once gave Tess Gallagher: Write a poem of ten lines in which you use six given words. Gallagher used five: *bruise, horse, milk, reason,* and *bride.* Here's the poem:

THE HORSE IN THE DRUGSTORE

wants to be admired.
He no longer thinks of what he has given up
to stand here, the milk-white reason
of chickens over his head in the night, the grass
spilling in through the day. No, it is enough
to stand so with his polished chest among the nipples
and bibs, the cotton and multiple sprays, with his black lips
parted just slightly and the forehooves doubled back

in the lavender air. He has learned here when maligned to snort dimes and to carry the inscrutable bruise like a bride.[9]

Of the poem's success, Marvin Bell observes that "it is a better poem for having been made to go somewhere—without knowing at the outset, where. One might venture that the best affliction for the young poet is a clear nearsightedness that nonetheless goes easily beyond the self."[10]

One way to make a poem go somewhere—without knowing where at the outset—is to ask questions about your subject. And one of the most effective poets ever to use the question as a literary form was God Himself when He wanted to cut Job down to size. God could have made His point with a series of statements. He could have said: "Job, I have commanded the morning and caused the dayspring to know his place. I have entered into the springs of the sea. The gates of death have opened unto Me and I have seen the doors of the shadow of death." But Job would have stopped listening. Answers are closed rooms; questions are open doors that invite us in. So God asked questions:

> 12 Hast thou commanded the morning since thy days; and caused the dayspring to know his place;
> 13 That it might take hold of the ends of the earth, that the wicked might be shaken out of it?
>
> . . . .
>
> 16 Hast thou entered into the springs of the sea? or hast thou walked in the search of the depth?
>
> . . . .
>
> 24 By what way is the light parted, which scattereth the east wind upon the earth?

. . . .

28 Hath the rain a father? or who hath begotten the drops
of dew?[11]

William Blake wanted to keep the tiger an open question and a
mystery when he wrote that famous poem in which every sentence is
a question. I give here the first three stanzas:

> Tyger Tyger, burning bright,
> In the forests of the night;
> What immortal hand or eye,
> Could frame thy fearful symmetry?
>
> In what distant deeps or skies,
> Burnt the fire of thine eyes?
> On what wings dare he aspire?
> What the hand dare seize the fire?
>
> And what shoulder, & what art,
> Could twist the sinews of thy heart?
> And when thy heart began to beat,
> What dread hand? & what dread feet?

Though these questions sound inevitable, they were not so easy
to ask. Early drafts show Blake asking them quite differently:

> stanza 2: Burnt in the distant deeps or skies
> The cruel fire of thine eyes
> Could heart descend or wings aspire
> What the hand dare seize the fire

> stanza 3: And when thy heart began to beat
> What dread hand and what dread feet
>
> Could fetch it from the furnace deep
> And in thy horrid ribs dare steep
> In the well of sanguine woe
> In what clay and in what mould
> Were thy eyes of fury rolled[12]

Such a mode of questioning would never stand up in court. Blake has already passed judgment on the tiger. The questions contain their own answers. What is the tiger? A cruel, horrid beast, a creature of sanguine woe. By the time he wrote his final draft Blake knew that the tiger is neither cruel nor horrid. The tiger simply is.

I suppose most of us take for granted the kinds of questions we are asked in ordinary life—exams, questionnaires—which is why we are so moved when a poet shapes them into a poem, as Denise Levertov does in "What Were They Like?" The poem takes place in the far future and has two speakers: the historian who inquires about the wholly destroyed, nearly mythical country of Vietnam; and the guide who answers, or fails to answer, six questions. "Did they use bone and ivory, / jade and silver, / for ornament?" asks the historian. And the guide answers: "A dream ago, perhaps. Ornament is for joy. / All the bones were charred." His last answer is a question: "Who can say? It is silent now."[13]

Marvin Bell's "Study Guide for the *Odyssey*" needs no comment. Anyone familiar with such guides will marvel at how the speaker uses the passionless questions of a study guide to raise the passionate questions of his own history.

1

Briefly,
in ten years what happened

before the story begins?
What does "odyssey" mean?

Identify Scylla and Charybdis.
Is this an epic?

Why ten years of war,
three of adventure

and seven with Calypso?
Is this an epic? Aristotle:

The romantic is wonderful
rather than probable.

2

Is there usually a feast or two,
a hero upon whom etc.,

a plea to the Muse for help?
Does Penelope handle her suitors?

What is the epithet?
Who lied—Odysseus or Homer?

Do we admire a trickster?
Is it hot where you lie reading

and are you aroused?
What does form "imitate"

and how?
Are you still beautiful?

3

Do you know a figure of speech
when you meet one?

Is it too far to you by now?
Is not this an epic

in which you have been lost?
Is Penelope so unlike Odysseus?[14]

The more poems you write, the more you discover that all statements are not created equal, that some lead to poems, some to conversation, and some to silence. To help my students find statements that lead to poetry, I sometimes ask them to write a "litany," that is, a poem in which every line is a statement opening with a set formula. Those I heard as a child led me to suppose that all litanies were impersonal, right minded, and well behaved, like this one:

O ye Sun and Moon, bless ye the Lord:
O ye Stars of heaven, bless ye the Lord:

O ye Showers and Dew, bless ye the Lord:

.   .   .   .

O ye Whales and all that move in the waters, bless ye the Lord:[15]

When a poet uses the litany for his own purposes and he praises
not the Lord but his cat or his mother, the poem seems to be addressed
to a crowd of listeners instead of a single reader. One can almost
hear the poet raising his voice to quiet them. When Christopher
Smart considers his cat in the litany form, he is not so much celebrat-
ing the cat—he could have accomplished that in a sonnet—as invok-
ing it:

> For I will consider my Cat Jeoffrey.
> For he is the servant of the Living God, duly and daily
>   serving him.
> For at the First glance of the glory of God in the East he
>   worships in his way.
> For is this done by wreathing his body seven times round
>   with elegant quickness.
> For then he leaps up to catch the musk, which is the bless-
>   ing of God upon his prayer.
> For he rolls upon prank to work it in.
> For having done duty and received blessing he begins to
>   consider himself.
> For this he performs in ten degrees.
> For first he looks upon his fore-paws to see if they are
>   clean.
> For secondly he kicks up behind to clear away there.
> For thirdly he works it upon stretch with the fore-paws
>   extended.

For fourthly he sharpens his paws by wood.

For fifthly he washes himself.

For sixthly he rolls upon wash.

For Seventhly he fleas himself, that he may not be interrupted upon the beat.

For Eighthly he rubs himself against a post.

For Ninthly he looks up for his instructions.

For Tenthly he goes in quest of food.

For having consider'd God and himself he will consider his neighbour.

For if he meets another cat he will kiss her in kindness.

For when he takes his prey he plays with it to give it a chance.

For one mouse in seven escapes by his dallying.

For when his day's work is done his business more properly begins.

For he keeps the Lord's watch in the night against the adversary.

How he counteracts the powers of darkness by his electrical skin and glaring eyes.

For he counteracts the Devil, who is death, by brisking about the life.

For in his morning orisons he loves the sun and the sun loves him.

For he is of the tribe of Tiger.

For the Cherub Cat is a term of the Angel Tiger.

For he has the subtlety and hissing of a serpent, which in goodness he suppresses.

For he will not do destruction, if he is well fed, neither will he spit without provocation.

For he purrs in thankfulness, when God tells him he's a
    good Cat.
For he is an instrument for the children to learn benevo-
    lence upon.
For every house is incomplete without him and a blessing is
    lacking in the spirit.[16]

Litanies always let you know, by the sound of them, that in their
youth they were part of those rituals that linked people to their past,
magically and spiritually. Litany *poems* remind me of a ritual our family
kept when I was growing up. Two weeks before Christmas, gifts would
slowly accumulate under the Christmas tree. But the gift I kept my
eye out for never arrived before Christmas Eve. It was marked with
my name and signed, "From the ancestors."

Inside I always found some object I'd known all my life: a silver
spoon, a pewter cup, a snuffbox, a bottle blown in the shape of a girl's
slipper. It was a gift from my ancestors because it had been handed
down from one generation to the next for so long that its first users
were unknown to me. Isn't a poem in the shape of a litany a kind of
gift from the ancestors as well—ancient, yet personal, and as immediate
as ourselves? The more personal the material it organizes, the greater
the tension between the public form and the private content. Here is
Linda Pastan's "Because"—as personal a litany as you are likely to
find anywhere:

> Because the night you asked me,
> the small scar of the quarter moon
> had healed—the moon was whole again;
> because life seemed so short;
> because life stretched before me

like the darkened halls of nightmare;
because I knew exactly what I wanted;
because I knew exactly nothing;
because I shed my childhood with my clothes—
they both had years of wear left in them;
because your eyes were darker than my father's;
because my father said I could do better;
because I wanted badly to say no;
because Stanley Kowalski shouted "Stella . . .";
because you were a door I could slam shut;
because endings are written before beginnings;
because I knew that after twenty years
you'd bring the plants inside for winter
and make a jungle we'd sleep in naked;
because I had free will;
because everything is ordained;
I said yes.[17]

Now take away the formula *because*, and you have a poem that reads much like a beautifully told story:

the night you asked me,
the small scar of the quarter moon
had healed—the moon was whole again;
life seemed so short;
life stretched before me
like the darkened halls of nightmare.

I have a bad habit of looking for stories in poems the way a lot of readers look for symbols. Perhaps, as habits go, it's not so bad as some, and perhaps the distinction between the storyteller and the poet is not as clear as we like to believe. In an essay called "Stories," Randall Jarrell writes,

> The poet or storyteller, so to speak, writes numbers on a blackboard, draws a line under them, and adds them into their true but unsuspected sum. . . .
>
> Stories can be as short as a sentence . . . The enlisted men at Fort Benning buried their dog Calculus under a marker that read: *He made better dogs of us all.* . . .
>
> When we try to make, out of these stories life gives us, works of art of comparable concision, we almost always put them into verse.[18]

What draws me into a poem that also happens to tell a story is never the plot. No, it is the teller, the witness, who gives direct testimony, not simply information. And I am drawn to this teller in poems that were not meant to tell stories at all. The more fantastic the events the teller has witnessed, the plainer I wish his account of them to be. When I first heard the opening lines of Henry Vaughan's poem "The World," I imagined a man coming in late to work and saying very quietly, by way of an excuse,

> I saw Eternity the other night
> Like a great *Ring* of pure and endless light,
> All calm, as it was bright,[19]

The rest of the poem, however, is not so much a story as a tapestry, or a story Vaughan lost the thread of in the maze of his own rhetoric. George Herbert and Emily Dickinson bear witness to eternity in a plain language that suits it better. In a letter Dickinson writes, "Were the Statement 'We shall not all sleep, but we shall all be changed,' made in earthly Manuscript, were his Residence in the Universe, we should pursue the Writer till he explained it to us."[20] When Emily Dickinson wants us to see eternity, she tells us a story.

> Because I could not stop for Death—
> He kindly stopped for me—
> The Carriage held but just Ourselves—
> And Immortality.
>
> We slowly drove—He knew no haste
> And I had put away
> My labor and my leisure too,
> For His Civility—
>
> We passed the School, where Children strove
> At Recess—in the Ring—
> We passed the Fields of Gazing Grain—
> We passed the Setting Sun—
>
> Or rather—He passed Us—
> The Dews drew quivering and chill—
> For only Gossamer, my Gown—
> My Tippet—only Tulle—
>
> We paused before a House that seemed
> A Swelling of the Ground—
> The Roof was scarcely visible—
> The Cornice—in the Ground—

Since then—'tis Centuries—and yet
Feels shorter than the Day
I first surmised the Horses' Heads
Were toward Eternity—[21]

I am sure when Emily Dickinson arrived in heaven, she was immediately named the patron saint of plain speech, the stern gatekeeper who makes adverbs state their business and sends many an idle adjective packing. Had a prophet or a saint told this story, we would call it a parable, but neither of these would have told it in the same way. In the New Testament, parables are told to teach people truths that they would otherwise find too obvious to hold their attention. The parables that poets write are more personal; Louis MacNeice calls them a form of "double-level writing." He observes:

One very valuable kind of parable, and particularly so today, is the kind which on the surface may not look like a parable at all. This is a kind of double-level writing, or, if you prefer, sleight-of-hand. . . . Mr. Eliot said that good verse should show the virtues of good prose. . . . [in] some modern parabolists, there is a . . . fundamental irony in the contrast between their . . . everyday mode of expression and their cosmic or mystical themes.[22]

This truth was never taught in the devil's school; it would make escape too easy. You remember the conditions set by the devil at the beginning of this essay: "Write a poem about the moon. If you pass the exam, the moon in your hand will disappear and you will find yourself back in the world from which you came." Now I am ready to take that exam. I will tell the moon a story. But before I do, let me preface my story with a few biographical facts. I am married to a photographer whose darkroom lies on the other side of our bedroom wall. If I go to bed first, I am lulled to sleep by his footsteps, his mutterings, his radio, and the low chatter of running water. One night I fell asleep with all these sounds about me and dreamed that I'd left the darkroom window open—a thing I never do in my waking hours, as it has no screen and attracts bats. But in the dream, open it stood, and something flew in. To my relief it was not a bat. It was the moon, who, shining into the window, mistook this fine and private place for a pocket in the great garment of the night, darkness within darkness and night within night. Many a story has its taproot hidden in a dream and many a poem also. Now I lay my hands on the moon and tell her my dream.

THE PHOTOGRAPHER AND THE MOON

The moon carries a black box
strapped to her back which she
turns on me.

Still, I leave her my room.
I open the window
and close the door.

When the moon flies in
I hear her running water
and opening her box.

Someone is taking baths,
one after another.
When I take out my dirty

pictures, showing her
self as a new moon,
she stops singing.

I turn my head.
What is that pulse,
that music too far

for the tune to carry,
like a grand ball
on the other side of the water?[23]

Nothing happens. I am about to protest, "But I'm telling you the truth, Moon. I really dreamed this," for I have sometimes asked storytellers if the events in their stories are true. But of the story itself, have I ever asked anything except that I believe it?

"Moon," I say, "I have found you out. You are as indifferent to me as the stones in the road. The moon of my childhood and the moon of my dreams are no brighter than the night light shaped like the moon in my son's room."

The sun is rising. As I tell my last story, I lay hands on the moon and feel it vanishing under my fingers, though whether the morning or myself has given it so faint a heart, I do not know.

NIGHT LIGHT

The moon is not green cheese.
It is china and stands in this room.
It has a ten-watt bulb and a motto:
Made in Japan.

Whey-faced, doll-faced.
it's closed as a tooth
and cold as the dead are cold
till I touch the switch.

Then the moon performs
its one trick:
it turns into a banana.
It warms to its subjects,

it draws us into its light
just as I knew it would
when I gave ten dollars
to the pale clerk

in the store that sold
everything.
She asked, Did I have a car?
She shrouded the moon in tissue

and laid it to rest in a box.
The box did not say Moon.

It said, This Side Up.
I tucked the moon into my basket

and bicycled into the world.
By the light of the sun
I could not see the
moon under my sack of apples,

moon under slab of salmon,
moon under clean laundry,
under milk its sister
and bread its brother,

moon under meat.
Now supper is eaten.
Now laundry is folded away.
I shake out the old comforters.

My nine cats take their places
and go on dreaming where they left off.
My son snuggles under the heap.
His father loses his way in a book.

It is time to turn on the moon.
It is time to live by a different light.[24]

NOTES

[1] Minou Drouet, poem, in "Proof of a Prodigy," *Life* 40:53 (13 Feb. 1956).

[2] Theodore Roethke, "The Teaching Poet," in *On the Poet and His Craft: Selected Prose of Theodore Roethke,* Ralph J. Mills, Jr., ed. (Seattle and London: University of Washington Press, 1979), 47–48.

[3] Pablo Neruda, "Ode to an Onion," in *Odas Elementales*, Carlos Lozano, trans. (New York: Las Americas Publishing Company, 1961), 27, 29.

[4] Gerard Manley Hopkins, journal entry, in *A Hopkins Reader*, John Pick, ed. (London: Oxford University Press, 1953), 53, 54, 57.

[5] Kevin Crossley-Holland, trans., *Storm and Other Old English Riddles* (New York: Farrar, Straus & Giroux, 1970), 58.

[6] Emily Dickinson, *Selected Poems of Emily Dickinson* (New York: The Modern Library, 1924), 125.

[7] Virginia Woolf, *The Waves* (London: Hogarth Press, 1931), 176.

[8] Randall Jarrell, "Poets, Critics and Readers," in *A Sad Heart at the Supermarket: Essays & Fables* (New York: Atheneum, 1967), 94.

[9] Tess Gallagher, "The Horse in the Drugstore," in Marvin Bell's "Homage to The Runner," *American Poetry Review* 7:6 (Nov./Dec. 1978): 12.

[10] Ibid., comment by Marvin Bell.

[11] Job 38:12–28.

[12] Martin K. Nurmi, "Blake's Revisions of *The Tyger*," *PMLA* 71:4 (Sept. 1956): 669–85.

[13] Denise Levertov, "What Were They Like?" in *The Sorrow Dance* (New York: New Directions, 1966), 84.

[14] Marvin Bell, "Study Guide for the *Odyssey*," *American Review* 25 (October 1976): 146–47.

[15] Hymn 633, *The Hymnal of The Protestant Episcopal Church in the United States of America* (New York: The Church Pension Fund, 1943), 715.

[16] This passage from "My Cat, Jeoffrey," with modernized spelling and punctuation, is included in *The Rattle Bag,* Seamus Heaney and Ted Hughes, eds. (London: Faber and Faber, 1982), 301–2. The original can be found in *Poems* by Christopher Smart, Robert Brittain, ed. (Princeton, New Jersey: Princeton University Press, 1950), 118.

[17] Linda Pastan, "Because," in *P.M/A.M* (New York: W. W. Norton & Company, 1982), 65.

[18] Randall Jarrell, "Stories," in *A Sad Heart at the Supermarket,* 146–48.

[19] Henry Vaughan, "The World," in *The Works of Henry Vaughan*, L. C. Martin, ed. (Oxford: Clarendon Press, 1957), 466.

[20] Emily Dickinson, *The Letters of Emily Dickinson*, Thomas H. Johnson, ed. (Cambridge, Mass.: The Belknap Press of Harvard University Press, 1951), 621.

[21] Emily Dickinson, "Because I Could Not Stop for Death," in *The Complete Poems of Emily Dickinson*, Thomas H. Johnson, ed. (Boston: Little, Brown & Company, 1960), 350.

[22] Louis MacNeice, *Varieties of Parable* (Cambridge University Press, 1965), 2–3, 46, 48.

[23] Nancy Willard, "The Photographer and the Moon," in *Household Tales of Moon and Water* (New York: Harcourt Brace Jovanovich, 1982), 29.

[24] Nancy Willard, "Night Light," in *Household Tales of Moon and Water*, 3.

WHEN BY NOW AND TREE BY LEAF:
TIME AND TIMELESSNESS
IN THE READING AND MAKING
OF CHILDREN'S BOOKS

• • • • • • • • •

I put on my dream-cap one day and . . . climbed the hill . . . , and there, on the tip-top, I found a house as old as the world itself.

That was where Father Time lived; and who should sit in the sun at the door, spinning away for dear life, but Time's Grandmother. . . .

"Good-morning," says Time's Grandmother to me.

"Good-morning," says I to her.

"And what do you seek here?" says she to me.

"I come to look for odds and ends," says I to her.

"Very well," says she; "just climb the stairs to the garret, and there you will find more than ten men can think about."

. . . .

Over in the corner was a great, tall clock, that had stood there silently with never a tick or a ting since men began to grow too wise for toys and trinkets.

But I knew very well that the old clock was the

Wonder Clock;

so down I took the key and wound it—gurr! gurr! gurr!

Click! buzz! went the wheels, and then—tick-tock! tick-tock! for the Wonder Clock is of that kind that it will never wear out, no matter how long it may stand in Time's garret."[1]

Not long ago I walked into a pharmacy and bought my first digital watch. I bought it out of necessity rather than desire; I was traveling and had forgotten my old one with its comfortable round face on which the numbers stood in a circle like children in a game. The clerk, seeing my misgivings, told me all the wonderful things this digital watch could do. It could tell time. It could tell the date. It could wake me at any hour of the day or night. It could do everything except make me immortal.

I took all these miracles on faith. A wonder clock, indeed! And I did not even know how to set it. But the watch I'd left at home was a wonder clock too. Long ago I had found it on the sidewalk in the last square of a faintly chalked game of hopscotch, the one that I always called Home. But this version had a cosmic dimension. In the last square was written *Heaven.* So it was in heaven that I found my watch. As with all gifts of the spirit, it had no warranty, no address to which I could send it for repairs.

Heaven seems the right place to find a watch when the finder never learned to tell time till she was in the seventh grade. All my classmates had mastered the intricacies of time in first grade, but sickness kept me out of school during the month that time was the subject, and by the time I realized what I didn't know, I was too shy to admit it. Recently a friend of mine told me that she will never forget the day she arrived at college as a freshman and met her roommate and, groping for conversation, asked her, "What time is it?" To her astonishment the girl burst into tears and confessed she had never learned to tell time. And my friend sat down with her and taught her on the spot. It might have comforted that girl if she had known that Emily Dickinson also did not learn to tell time till she was old enough to know better.

Telling time is so simple for children now. They do not need to *tell* anything. They read out the numbers on their digital watches. And surely their experience of time is very different from that for those of us who were brought up among clocks with old-fashioned dials. For us, time is space. An hour is as round and friendly as the full moon, which often peeps through a tiny window on the dials of grandfather clocks. A quarter of an hour is a quarter of a pie, wherein the minutes nestle as closely knit as cells in a comb, and if they are joyful, every cell is filled with honey, and if they are dull, they stand empty and flavorless as wax. To the digital generation, I suppose time is linear. The minutes fall away, never to be heard from again. There is no record of the past and no promise of the future, only the swiftly vanishing present.

Time is money, an uncle of mine told me once. He was a broker, so I suppose for him this was true. Once, standing in line at the bank and glancing impatiently at my watch, I heard what sounded like whispering: the sound of bills rustling through the tellers' fingers. I had often been told that money talks, but not until then did I hear the conspiratorial whispering of money talking to itself. The image of time as a flutter of bills and a chiming of small change rises up in my mind when I wear my digital watch, which counts minutes as impalpable as air that has had all the weather conditioned out of it.

Such is not the time I live by.

The old Chinese way of measuring time has always seemed closer to the skin of things than ours. Take the hours, for example. The day begins at midnight and is divided into two-hour watches, each bearing the name of an animal. From twelve A.M. till two P.M. is the hour of the rat. From two till four A.M. is the hour of the ox. What an advantage for poets! You could say of your hero, "He was born in the hour of the tiger," with perfect accuracy. Instead of "They met at seven in the evening," you could say of star-crossed lovers, "They met at the hour of the dragon," and no one would mistake measure for metaphor.

Or take the months, as the Sioux measured them, in moons: the moon of falling leaves (October), the moon when the calf grows hair (September), the moon of the snow-blind (March), the moon of the grass appearing (April). How intimately your sense of time would connect you with grass and leaves and snow if your calendar were to be found between the lines of the book of nature.

And surely this is how children know time, even after they've learned the use of watches. I remember when my son was small, and I was waiting for the school bus with him early in the morning. A whole flock of children waited with us, and on that particular morning the bus was late. Though nobody had a watch, everybody had a sense of the time, and one child observed, "It smells like the bus is late this morning." Translated, this means: The air is not as cool, not as fresh, not as quiet, at a quarter of nine as it is at eight-thirty. Different birds sing. More cars pass—and more slowly.

Before I learned to tell time, I relied almost entirely on this method and found it remarkably accurate. During the summer, how easy it was to lay time aside, along with my workbooks and readers. When

I was small, I spent my summers in a cottage just outside the village of Oxford, Michigan. My mother, my sister, and I stayed here from June to September, and my father, who taught summer school at the university, joined us on the weekends. Only on weekends did we have the use of a car.

In the living room we had one outlet and three appliances: a toaster, a radio, and a clock. You could have news or you could have time or you could have toast. You could not have all three at once. When a neighbor brought us a jar of her homemade elderberry jam, we did without news and time altogether—until we ran out of bread. Sometimes a man came around in a truck midweek, selling bread, but mostly he didn't. Sometimes we walked into town, telling ourselves that bread was the object of our expedition but knowing that it was only the flimsiest of pretexts for travel. We went not for bread but for adventure. A trip into town took nearly the whole day. First we rowed across the lake. Then we crossed a pasture, keeping a sharp eye out for bulls. Then we slogged along the highway till the sidewalk and shade trees appeared. After we'd crossed the tracks, a sign told us that we had passed the city limits. We bought our bread and a newspaper, we had ice cream at the soda fountain in the drugstore, and we stopped at the dime store for a laying-on of hands: touching the toys, the souvenirs, the sets of dishes—all matching, without chips or cracks. On the way home we stopped in the pasture to rest, where Mother spread out the newspaper for me to lie on, since the grass was full of thistles.

And time? It was not so much measured as observed. When you cannot read the time in numbers, you read it in experience: autumn, winter, spring, summer, sun, moon, stars, rain. Day when the dandelion leaves are no longer tender enough to use in salad. Day when the first daylilies bloom. Day when the first milkweed pods ripen and brightness falls from the air. Day when the goatsbeard no longer flowers. And one night the stars come earlier, and the next night earlier still, and it is time to go back to school.

I recognized this way of learning to tell time by the closing of a petal rather than the passing of an hour when I first came across the following poem by e. e. cummings. It seemed as if I were watching the play of Everyman, or, as the poet calls his characters, "anyone" and his wife "noone," who live out their lives in time among their neighbors, the someones and the everyones:

anyone lived in a pretty how town
(with up so floating many bells down)
spring summer autumn winter
he sang his didn't he danced his did.

Women and men (both little and small)
cared for anyone not at all
they sowed their isn't they reaped their same
sun moon stars rain

children guessed (but only a few
and down they forgot as up they grew
autumn winter spring summer)
that noone loved him more by more

when by now and tree by leaf
she laughed his joy she cried his grief
bird by snow and stir by still
anyone's any was all to her

someones married their everyones
laughed their cryings and did their dance
(sleep wake hope and then) they
said their nevers they slept their dream

stars rain sun moon
(and only the snow can begin to explain
how children are apt to forget to remember
with up so floating many bells down)

one day anyone died i guess
(and noone stooped to kiss his face)
busy folk buried them side by side
little by little and was by was

all by all and deep by deep
and more by more they dream their sleep
noone and anyone earth by april
wish by spirit and if by yes.

Women and men (both dong and ding)
summer autumn winter spring
reaped their sowing and went their came
sun moon stars rain[2]

Anyone who has learned to tell time late has a certain difficulty
in separating past from present; like loving friends, they go hand in
hand. This was especially true for me, since I loved to read. While
my visible mortal part was hunched over a book in Michigan, my spirit
was off questing in London, in Africa, in ancient Egypt, in Oz. I would

emerge from the past or the future, sleepy-eyed, into the present, as one who has been under a long enchantment.

Story and history—this is how I came to understand time in the literature I read as a child.

I did not fall in love with history the way some children fall in love with dinosaurs or knights in armor or the Civil War. I liked the past only when it was as concrete as the present, and I used to think it would be wonderful if history could be taught by ghosts. The ghost of Queen Elizabeth. The ghost of George Washington. They would come in and we would ask them to tell us important things that the history books forgot. "Queen Elizabeth, what did you eat for breakfast?" "George Washington, were you ever afraid of the dark?"

Years later I found that history could tell me these things if only I went to the books that let the dead speak for themselves. When I studied medieval history, I forgot the battles and remembered the lively banter of Chaucer's pilgrims and the still, small voices of the anonymous poets whose songs have come down to us scribbled in the margins of sermons and other edifying and forgotten works. This song, for example, from the fourteenth century, reprinted in Helen Cooper's *Great Grandmother Goose:*

> I am of Ireland,
> and of the holy land
> of Ireland.
>
> Good sir, pray I thee,
> for Saint Charity,
> come and dance with me
> in Ireland.

> I am of Ireland.
> and of the holy land
> of Ireland.[3]

The invitation must have been irresistible to the priest sitting in his study, listening to the folk singing and dancing on Saturday night, and he with his sermon to prepare. In a handbook for priests, *Gemma Ecclesiastica,* written in the sixteenth century, we find this description of the consequences:

> There was an instance of a priest in the region of Worcester, England, in our own time, who heard throughout the whole night that section of a song called the refrain, the part which is repeated over and over. It was being sung by a group of dancers outside the church. Next morning when the priest stood at the altar, vested and signed with the cross, instead of the salutation, "The Lord be with you," he sang out in a loud voice, in English, the refrain: . . . . "My sweetest friend, your lover desires your favors."
> This incident was the reason why the bishop of the place . . . prohibited . . . that that song be sung for the remainder of his episcopacy.[4]

And what of the nuns? What distractions had they? The injunction sent to Romsey Abbey by William of Wykenham in 1387 gives me the very texture of life in that convent, a merrier place, by all reports, than the convent that my husband's aunt entered fifty years ago in Mount Pleasant, Michigan:

Item, whereas we have convinced ourselves by clear proofs that some of the nuns of your house bring with them to church birds, rabbits, hounds and such like frivolous things, whereunto they give more heed than to the offices of the church, with frequent hindrance to their own psalmody and to that of their fellow nuns and to the grievous peril of their souls—therefore we strictly forbid you all and several, in virtue of the obedience due to us that ye presume henceforward to bring to church no birds, hounds, rabbits or other frivolous things that promote indiscipline. . . . The alms that should be given to the poor are devoured and the church and cloister . . . are foully defiled . . . and . . . through their inordinate noise divine service is frequently troubled. . . .[5]

It was in the back rooms of history, not in the parlor, that I met Tittivillus, the devil specially appointed to collect the syllables dropped by nuns who gabbled too quickly through their prayers. It was in the kitchens of history that I discovered the herbs in my kitchen were old, distinguished guests, with their roots in a distant, magical past. It was from the cooks in those kitchens that I learned how to time one's dishes by repeating prayers: a pudding by a paternoster and an egg by a miserere. The medieval cook could not tell time either, yet ignorance did not keep him from preparing many a fine feast.

Several years ago my son asked me if I knew anybody who was alive during the Second World War, and from the way he asked it, I knew that the Second World War was as distant to him as the Crusades are to me.

"There are people on our street who remember the war very well," I assured him. "Go and ask them about it."

There is no better way to discover the secret pasts of your neighbors than to send out a small boy with a tape recorder. Like a young Studs Terkel, he made his own oral history of the war. His witnesses included a Frenchman, a German, an American Jew, and an Armenian news photographer. Here was history, alive in the mouths of those who had lived it. The past became present, as it almost always does in oral histories. No summary of dates and events can match the details and the idioms of the speakers themselves. Let the timid storytellers among us never forget the value of their own history, the story that answers the question, What did you do when you were little like me? Lucky the child who is given a book of oral history, such as Alvin Schwartz's *When I Grew Up Long Ago* or Carol Ann Bales's *Tales of the Elders,* and told that he too can be a gatherer of time, a musician of lost voices.

One of the most vivid images I know occurs in an interview with an elderly black man in Georgia, taken down in the thirties and forties by a woman who wanted to save not only the facts of local history but the idiom that flavored it. Here is Wright Boyer's account of how the devil got thrown out of eternal joy into eternal torment:

The Devil was plenty smart back in the old days, and bless your time, he was one of the greatest songsters in heaven. Surely was. He used to lead the singing choir up there in heaven and sometime he would hop up on a pole and whistle just like a mockingbird. There just wasn't any stopping him. He used to issue out the blessing three times a day amongst the other angels up there, and he named himself Champion Luther. If ever there was a sight, he was one.

Then he got to cutting up powerful bad; said if he didn't take that kingdom, he was going to build a kingdom to the north side of that one about a span above the stars. And that proves it was a starry heaven. Um-m-m-hum! Um-m-m-hum!

·   Well, then, after he had done all that talking, he up and banished himself. After a while Michael was standing by the Royal where God was seated and he looked out and saw the Devil coming back and he said, "Behold! The great dragon is coming to take vengeance on our kingdom, all-stained-in-hallowed blood."

And when he got there the Devil raised a war. He fought and cut up scandalous and backed the angels up under the throne. God was sitting there watching from the Royal.

After then the Devil disappeared again. And when he had come back Michael looked out and saw him again. And he said, "Be-HO-O-OLD! The great dragon is a coming again!"

God didn't say anything to Michael the other time, but this time He said, "Michael, you go out and meet him and put him out of here. If you have to reach back there in my wardrobe and take seven bolts of thunder and put against him. Put him out of here, Michael! Put him out!"

God was just sitting on the Royal watching to see what was going to happen. Michael grabbed the Devil and the Lord told him to put him out. Michael threw the Devil over the banister of time. Then he tipped over and peeped way down and saw the Devil where he had dropped to and he said, "Lord, the great dragon fell way down to torment."[6]

If anyone had asked the teller of this tale to write a story, very likely he could not have done it. Is there something in the process of telling of stories that gives us the freedom to let the tale unwind on the spool of language? I have known students who were afraid of writing because they were afraid of failing, but when they told stories, they were afraid of nothing. Storyteller Donald Davies took a group of fourth and fifth graders who had trouble writing and worked with them intensively on storytelling, with startling results. He started out by telling them stories, simple stories at first, then longer tales, more complex but similar in form. From hearing stories they went on to telling stories. Davies was well pleased with the results of his experiment. The children's stories were neither random nor disorganized but followed the archetypal patterns of the stories they had heard. Says Davies: "They brought their own content, and now that content had form. . . . Now they could not only tell a well-organized story, but were able to organize their work better in study areas far removed from storytelling."[7]

I believe that listening to stories and telling stories sharpens our awareness of language, of what we mean when we tell a student, "Find your own voice as a writer." It is sometimes a revelation to children to hear different versions of the same story. Take, for example, Beatrix Potter's own telling of the adventures of Peter Rabbit and Benjamin Bunny. Surely children, who often think that published writers write books by magic with no more effort than it takes to lift a pen, would find her remarks on writing both surprising and comforting: "My usual way of writing is to scribble, and cut out, and write it again and

again. . . . I polish, polish, polish! to the last, revise."[8] Here is a passage
from *The Tale of Benjamin Bunny:*

> One morning a little rabbit sat on a bank.
>
> He pricked his ears and listened to the trit-trot, trit-
> trot of a pony.
>
> A gig was coming along the road; it was driven by Mr.
> McGregor, and beside him sat Mrs. McGregor in her best
> bonnet.
>
> As soon as they had passed, little Benjamin Bunny slid
> down into the road, and set off—with a hop, skip, and a
> jump—to call upon his relations, who lived in the wood at
> the back of Mr. McGregor's garden.[9]

And here is the scene as recounted in *Benjamin Bunny Visits Peter
Rabbit,* retold by Corey Nash for *The Little Treasury of Peter Rabbit:* "One
morning Benjamin Bunny sat on a bank. He heard a pony and carriage
coming along the road; it was driven by Mr. McGregor and beside
him sat Mrs. McGregor. As soon as they had passed, Benjamin slid
down into the road to call upon his cousin, Peter Rabbit."[10]

A number of things have gone out of the original passage. First,
the sound: the trit-trot, trit-trot of the pony's hooves on the road. The
nonsense syllables re-creating the sound of those hooves are as necessary
to our enjoyment of the scene as the nonsense refrains that tumble
through the songs of Mother Goose: "hickety, pickety, my black hen";
"hickory, dickory, dock"; "hey diddle diddle"; "rub-a-dub-dub." In
poetry and stories that are meant to be heard, sense and nonsense are
the most amiable of friends, always at each other's service.

Second, the pleasures of an interesting vocabulary. *Gig* is an unfamiliar word, yet I think children could figure out what it means and have the pleasure of learning a new word that, to my taste, is more fun to say than *carriage*. And Potter's advice to herself is good advice for any writer: "I think the great point in writing for children is to have something to say and to say it in simple direct language."[11]

Third, the visual detail. There is no picture of Mrs. McGregor in her best bonnet, so unless I know the original story I shall never see that bonnet. And yet how much it tells us about this woman, for whom going to town is an event worthy of her best bonnet, along with Sunday morning services and weddings and funerals.

Yet a fourth element is lost: the pacing. Time does not pass at the same speed for all people and in all places, no matter how often clocks and schedules try to convince us differently. Nash's summary of events is no substitute for the experience of sitting on that bank with Benjamin Bunny, listening with ears pricked, to the trit-trot of the pony's hooves. "As soon as they had passed," Potter's version runs, "little Benjamin Bunny slid down into the road and set off—with a hop, a skip, and a jump—to call upon his relations, who lived in the wood at the back of Mr. McGregor's garden." All this takes time—the invisible but important character in every well-told story.

Listening to stories and telling stories give us immediate entry into the fourth dimension. Like us, they unfold in time; sequence and suspense is their flesh and blood. But time is money—a common currency, yet nobody I know has enough of it, and plenty of people would prefer to spend it on activities other than storytelling. Recently I discovered two collections of stories designed to meet this problem. The first is called *My Bedtime Book of Two-Minute Stories,* edited by Rosemary Garland, who in her preface describes the need for her book as follows:

"Tell me a bedtime story" is a cry that can bring dismay to even the most well-meaning mother, especially as it always seems to come when patience is at an end and minutes seem like hours. *My Bedtime Book of Two-Minute Stories* is designed to fill the needs of the child at such a moment, without stretching the adult's good humor to its limits. Here are fifty-eight stories, each of which will take but two minutes to read. . . . With *My Bedtime Book of Two-Minute Stories* in hand, you can afford to spoil your children. Don't read them one story, read them two![12]

For the very impatient, very tired mother (and it's interesting to note that Ms. Garland assumes the mother will tell the story, not the father), there is an even more efficient solution: *One-Minute Bedtime Stories,* by Shari Lewis. Her remarks on the need for such a book follow along the line of Ms. Garland's. In her preface to the stories, Ms. Lewis writes:

Many of our basic children's stories are well worth passing on as part of our cultural heritage. The only catch is this: These tales were written in another time, when life was lived at a slower pace, with fewer distractions and fewer available forms of entertainment. In their long form, the classic stories often don't fit our present needs.

That's why I started writing one-minute stories. And you can read these through in a minute, if you've had a rough day or if you're expecting ten people for dinner. On the other hand, you can stretch each tale into a five- or ten-minute shared experience . . . by looking at the art and asking your child "What if . . ." questions. "What would have happened if that boy had not cried, 'Wolf!' so many times before?"[13]

The story Ms. Lewis cites as bringing down the patience of a weary parent is "The Gingerbread Boy." "Your youngster (having heard this story before) won't let you miss a single detail, and by the eighth page about the runaway cookie, you're willing to do him in yourself!"[14] While sympathizing with the parent in this situation, not for worlds would I deprive a child of the pleasures of repetition. Like repetition in poetry, the gingerbread man's saucy challenge is not simply redundant, it is incantation. Can you imagine the story of Bluebeard without the repeated cry, "Ann, Sister Ann, do you see nothing coming?"

We live in a world where for many of us incantation has lost the power it had for our ancestors. But it has not lost its power for children. I know a father who, when his son was small, told him every night episodes in a continuing story about a giant bat. This father is a poet, who knows a good deal about language, sound, and repetition. Though he told the story in what he thought was ordinary speech, it was not ordinary to the child, who asked him eagerly every night, "Daddy, sing the giant bat."

And therein lies a clue as to where the best one-minute bedtime stories can be found. Collections of traditional ballads will give you enough stories, both comic and tragic, to last a lifetime. For sheer economy in the telling, few stories can equal the ballad of "Sir Patrick Spence," though I don't think I'd recommend it for bedtime:

> The king sits in Dumferling toune,
>   Drinking the blude-reid wine:
> "O whar will I get guid sailor,
>   To sail this schip of mine?"

Up and spak an eldern knicht,
    Sat at the kings richt kne:
"Sir Patrick Spence is the best sailor,
    That sails upon the se."

The king has written a braid letter,   *braid:* broad, official?
    And signed it wi' his hand,
And sent it to Sir Patrick Spence,
    Was walking on the sand.

The first line that Sir Patrick red,
    A loud lauch lauched he;
The next line that Sir Patrick red,
    The teir blinded his ee.

"O wha is this has done this deid,
    This ill deid don to me,
To send me out this time o' the yeir,
    To sail upon the se?!

"Mak hast, mak hast, my mirry men all,
    Our guid schip sails the morne:"
"O say na sae, my master deir,
    For I feir a deadlie storme.

"Late late yestreen I saw the new moone,
    Wi' the auld moone in hir arme,
And I feir, I feir, my deir master,
    That we will cum to harme."

O our Scots nobles were richt laith
    To weet their cork-heild schoone;
Bot lang owre a' the play wer playd,
    Thair hats they swam aboone.

O lang, lang, may their ladies sit,
    Wi' thair fans into their hand,
Or eir they se Sir Patrick Spence
    Cum sailing to the land.

O lang, lang, may the ladies stand,
    Wi' thair gold kems in their hair,
Waiting for their ain deir lords,
    For they'll se thame na mair.

Have owre, have owre to Aberdour,
    It's fiftie fadom deip,
And thair lies guid Sir Patrick Spence,
    Wi' the Scots lords at his feit.[15]

This ballad is older than verifiable history; it is ancient. I asked my students, What is the difference between old and ancient? Old was—well, as old as your grandmother. But ancient was really old, time out of mind. Ancient time was as old as myth. "In 1936, King Edward VIII gave up his throne to marry Mrs. Wallis Simpson" becomes "Once upon a time there was a king who loved a woman so much that he gave up everything for her, including his throne."

"Once upon a time" is outside of "ordinary time." And ordinary time is where most of us live most of the time. I borrow the term from a calendar published by a local gravestone company. Of course it doesn't call itself a gravestone company: It advertises monuments, markers, eternal-tribute memorials. Some of the date numerals on the calendar are red, some are purple, some are black—to mark the church season or saint's day. The green numbers represent ordinary time. In ordinary time, the digital days pass; they are not joined by ceremony or memory to the past or the future. This is the time of which the psalmist sings: "For a thousand years in thy sight are but as yesterday when it is past, and as a watch in the night. Thou carriest them away as with a flood; they are as a sleep: in the morning they are like grass which groweth up. In the morning it flourisheth . . . ; . . . in the evening it is cut down and withereth. . . . We spend our years as a tale that is told."[16]

But myths and fairy tales are merciful. They take us into another kind of time. Australian bushpeople call it the dreamtime. In dreamtime the past is present, and out of sight does not mean out of mind. And we need both kinds of time—the measurable time of history and the magic time of myth—just as we need both the scientific and the mythic answers to the questions children ask.

Ask me about questions and I'll tell you that questions are better company than answers just as open doors are better than closed doors—unless you are in danger of being robbed or freezing to death. Never was I so aware of the many answers a single question may have as when my son was small and asking the kinds of questions children have asked since the beginning of language. I shall never forget his first question: Where does the sun go at night? Many years before, I'd asked my father that question. My father was a scientist. He fetched a grapefruit and half a dozen oranges.

"This," he said, holding up the grapefruit, "is the sun."

Then he picked up an orange. "And this is the earth."

I was astonished. I had thought the sun was made of fire and the earth was made of rock. Remembering my father's citrus cosmology, I read of the World Tree in Norse mythology with a sense of déjà vu. Now, when my son asked that same question, I answered him differently.

"Where do you think it goes?" I asked.

"Oh, the sun finds a train," he assured me, "and the train goes into the ground, and the sun goes into the dining car and eats orange pie all night long to keep his color, so he won't be all pale when he comes up again."

His answer was as new as he was and as old as the Egyptian myth that answers the same question: On the primordial abyss of waters, through a great darkness, sails a boat that carries the sun. Instead of Amtrak, we have the Boat of Ra, also called the Boat of Millions of Years. Instead of stations, conductors, and commuters, we have the twelve goddesses of the night, the dangers and guardians of the underworld, and the grateful dead, traveling to salvation.

I made my son's answer into a picture book for him to show him that it was as valuable in its own way as the scientific answer. Of such answers are the oldest stories made. As my son has grown I have tried to give him both kinds, knowing that in a time-ridden age we need the timeless answer, the still small voice of the story.

NOTES

[1] Howard Pyle, Preface, *The Wonder Clock* (New York: Dover, 1965), v–vi.

[2] e. e. cummings, "anyone lived in a pretty how town," in *Poems 1923–1954* (New York: Harcourt Brace & World, Inc., 1959), 370–71.

[3] Helen Cooper, *Great Grandmother Goose* (New York: Greenwillow, 1978).

[4] John J. Hagen, trans., *Gerald of Wales The Jewel of the Church* (California: Lugduni Batavorum E. J. Brill MCMLXXIX, 1979), 92.

5 Eileen Power, *Mediaeval People* (New York: Barnes & Noble, 1971), 91.

6 Rose Thompson, collector, "The Devil," in *Hush, Child! Can't You Hear the Music?,* Charles Beaumont, ed. (Athens: University of Georgia Press, 1982), 2–4.

7 Donald Davies, "Storytelling and Comprehension Skills—A Classroom Experiment," *The Yarnspinner* 6: 12 (Dec. 1982): 1–2.

8 Leslie Lindner, *History of the Writings of Beatrix Potter* (London: Warne, 1971), xxv.

9 Beatrix Potter, *The Tale of Benjamin Bunny* (New York: F. Warne, 1904), 9.

10 Beatrix Potter, *Benjamin Bunny Visits Peter Rabbit,* retold by Corey Nash in *The Little Treasury of Peter Rabbit* (New York: Chatham River Press, 1983).

11 Lindner, xxv.

12 Rosemary Garland, Preface, *My Bedtime Book of Two-Minute Stories* (New York: Grosset & Dunlap, 1969), 7.

13 Shari Lewis, Preface, *One-Minute Bedtime Stories* (Garden City, New York: Doubleday, 1982), 6.

14 Ibid.

15 Albert B. Friedman, ed., "Sir Patrick Spence," *The Viking Book of Folk Ballads of the English-Speaking World* (New York: The Viking Press, 1956), 298–99.

16 Psalm 90:4–9.

NEWBERY MEDAL

ACCEPTANCE

FOR

A VISIT TO WILLIAM BLAKE'S INN:

POEMS FOR INNOCENT AND

EXPERIENCED TRAVELERS,

ILLUSTRATED BY

ALICE AND MARTIN PROVENSEN

• • • • • • • • •

The Provensens and I would like to thank the members of the Newbery and Caldecott committees for honoring our book and to thank everyone at Harcourt Brace Jovanovich with whom we worked. And we are especially glad for an opportunity to honor the remarkable woman who brought us together and who has seen me through ten books: Barbara Lucas.

When I was a child, I often heard it said that "little pitchers have big ears," and I knew in my heart that if I turned into a pitcher, no other pitcher in this world or out of it would have bigger ears than mine. I was luckier than many eavesdroppers. I spent part of my childhood in a house that had a party line. There were seven people on the line, and each household had its own ring. Ours was four short and one long. My mother made it clear to my sister and me that when the telephone rang for somebody else only very ill-bred people lifted up the receiver and listened in on other people's conversations.

One afternoon I was alone in the house, and the telephone rang: three short rings. The bell did not toll for us. A terrible curiosity overcame me. I lifted the receiver and heard a concert of clicks, like claws scampering over a bare floor: the sound of five other ill-bred people lifting up their receivers to listen in. I held my breath. Now I would find out how the world conducted itself when children were not keeping watch over it.

A voice that sounded as far away as Australia exclaimed, "And they had cloth napkins, with *Briarcroft Inn* printed in the corner."

"You don't mean it," purred the voice of Mrs. Johnson, who lived three houses down from ours.

"I could only get five of them in my purse," said the voice from Australia.

And then, with a flourish of chimes, the Good Humor man turned into our street, and both speakers and listeners hung up and ran out to meet him.

I did not know exactly what an inn was and supposed it was a place that had to take people in. If there was no room at the inn, you got the stable, which was guaranteed to hold a mother, a father, a child, shepherds, three kings, a company of angels, and a lot of animals. An inn was a place of great mercy and variety where no one was ever put out.

That evening I asked my mother, "What is an inn?"

"It's a resting place for travelers," she said, "like a hotel, only friendlier. Your father and I stayed in a wonderful inn on our honeymoon in a very small town in Germany. I remember when we got off the steamer, the porter met us and put all our luggage on his bicycle."

I felt a flood of sympathy for the porter.

"Were you the only people at the inn?" I asked.

"No, indeed. A great many interesting people stayed there. And the rooms were over a hundred years old."

"How did you know they were over a hundred years old?"

"Because our guide said so," answered my mother, "and because there were so many cracks in the plaster."

A resting place for interesting people, cracks in the plaster—if this was an inn, then all my life I had lived in one without knowing it. Surely no other inn had cracks in the plaster to match ours. Finding pictures in them was like looking for creatures in the shifting shapes of clouds. Whenever a new crack appeared, I fetched my box of paints, and my mother and I discussed the possibilities.

"What do you think it looks like? A whale?" I suggest.

"Yes, but do we really need a whale in the guest room?" asks Mother. "Couldn't you turn it into an angel, like the one you painted over the crack in the bathroom?"

And so in guest room and bathroom and crumbling hall, the patient angels went about their bright business, and the cracks went unobserved, for who looks at plaster in the presence of angels?

As for guests, nobody could ask for a greater variety than ours. On the third floor lived my grandfather, whose room held his clothes, his chewing tobacco, and the books he counted among his special friends: the Bible, *Pilgrim's Progress,* treatises on beekeeping and osteopathy, and the works of Edgar Allan Poe. When I came home from school, I could hear his voice rolling through the house, breathing life into the raven, Annabel Lee, and the tintinnabulation of the bells. After my grandfather moved out, my cousin, a sophomore at the local teachers college, dropped by one evening and told us he'd had a fight with his mother; could he please spend the night with us? He stayed six months.

A week after my cousin moved in, his best friend had a fight with *his* mother and moved in also. Unlike the rest of us, who enjoyed our creature comforts, they converted their beds to pallets on the floor and atoned for their sins with loud prayers, which started at six in the morning and stopped when the two penitents left for their eight o'clock class. Scarcely had the door closed behind them when my grandmother began humming and stirring in the room below theirs. From morning till evening she talked to herself, to the quick, and to the dead.

"Get the ladders ready, I got five men coming to pick cherries!" she would call to the hired man who had died fifty years before but who once sowed and slaughtered on her father's farm in Iowa. At night her English slipped away, and she recited prayers in German and dreamed herself back in that country church where the women sat on the left side and the men on the right and they heard about the wages of sin while an occasional wise cow waited outside like a visitor from a more peaceable kingdom.

Reading, drawing, doing my homework, I listened and noted in the margins of my books and math papers and class schedules whatever seemed worth the saving: a fragment of speech, a line of poetry. Years later, I was reading the poetry of William Carlos Williams and suddenly felt that he was speaking directly to me. "What do I do?" wrote Williams. "I listen. . . . This is my entire occupation."

And I would add: The poet writes poems for people to listen to, poems to be heard as well as read. Skipping rope or trading taunts on the jungle gym, children know the importance of hearing and saying poetry. But do we ever really outgrow that wish to hear a story, to say a poem? The babysitters and teachers who read to me have gone the way of all flesh, and I have had to make do with recordings of poems and stories played on a small portable phonograph, which I move from room to room while doing my housework. Scrubbing a floor is child's play if you can listen to Ralph Richardson reading William Blake.

One night, after the laundry was folded away and the floors swept, I stacked half a dozen grocery cartons in the living room and started to build a house in which wishing did the washing and magic did the mending. Here nobody kept house. The only thing anyone kept was the secret.

I knew my handmade house was going to be an inn when it started attracting guests. Every afternoon our plump cat climbed into the cardboard dining room and quite literally brought down the house. A friend who earned his living building real houses witnessed this awful spectacle and said, "Let me copy the house for you in wood." He took the measurements and a month later appeared with a tall wooden structure on his truck.

"Now paint it," he said.

Was it this habit of mixing poetry with housework that made me take the inn for a subject when Barbara Lucas asked me to write a collection of poems for children? Although I had been listening to Blake's poetry, I knew two editions of his poems from my childhood: *Songs of Innocence* and *Songs of Experience*, with Blake's pictures; and a selection of those songs called *The Land of Dreams*, illustrated by Pamela Bianco. What interested me as much as her drawings was her letter to Blake, which opens the book:

Dear Mr. Blake,

When I was first asked to make these drawings, it made me very happy because I had known and liked your poems for a long while. . . . yet when the opportunity at last presented itself, I began to get scared. . . . For, since you had made your drawings so well, I knew that nobody had any business to attempt to make different ones. And then I consoled myself by thinking that if I wrote and explained the whole thing to you, you would understand, and perhaps, after all, you wouldn't mind so very much.[1]

Since Pamela Bianco had written a letter to Blake, then surely somewhere, somehow, Blake was alive and could read it. Many years after I'd laid her book aside, I was attending a panel discussion at Princeton on the state of the arts and was startled to hear one of the panelists, Allen Ginsberg, quietly remark, "The last time I talked with William Blake . . ."

And now I find myself making the same statement. The last time I talked with William Blake I was wrestling with the problem of how to move the inn to Philadelphia for this conference, and I had just lost my glasses.

"You can get a new pair of glasses," said my son.

"No, I can't. Those frames belonged to my father before he died. They're irreplaceable."

That night I dreamed myself on a country road, driving a horse hitched to an open wagon. On the wagon rode my homemade house, William Blake's Inn. All at once the heavens opened, and the rains came, and when the air cleared and the sun returned I discovered to my horror that the inn had vanished. And who was this small man on a bicycle, gliding toward me? He was, I was sure, none other than William Blake. In my dream I burst into tears.

"Oh, Mr. Blake," I wailed, "I've lost your inn."

He pedaled more slowly, but he did not dismount.

"You haven't lost it," he assured me. "You've just lost sight of it. Be good to my guests. They're irreplaceable. Birds, beasts, air, water, flowers, grass. Me. You."

NOTES

[1] Pamela Bianco, ed., Preface, *The Land of Dreams: Twenty Poems by William Blake* (New York: Macmillan, 1928), 3.

THE BIRDS AND THE BEASTS
WERE THERE:
AN INTERVIEW WITH MARTIN
PROVENSEN

* * * * * * * * *

Past chicory, goldenrod, and Queen Anne's lace nodding on both sides of this road that winds through the backwoods of Dutchess County; past the nature camp where my son spent so many summers; through the gate and past the pond, as flat and tidy as a carpet in the green meadow; past the horse browsing and the gray geese posing like Chinese porcelains; past the gray barn—and now Martin and Alice have heard our car, and they come out of the farmhouse, which so many children who have never made this journey know well. This is Maple Hill Farm.

A flock of chickens the color of butterscotch rush up to inspect us. Their legs are feathered right down to their toes; they appear to be wearing pantaloons, though my husband, Eric, says they look like

Sherpa guides from the Himalayas, and Martin tells us that this particular species comes from China.

"I saw them at the county fair and got some for the farm," he
explains. "These are still young chicks. They will be twice as large
when they're grown."

Half a dozen more-familiar black hens bustle past us, pursuing
important business in the vegetable garden.

"We call them the Thurbers," Alice remarks, "because Thurber
writes so well about hens."

The name suits them perfectly. Beyond the vegetable garden lies
the jungle, from which an occasional fox comes to carry off an occasional hen.

Because we have arrived late, we go directly into the kitchen for
lunch and seat ourselves at the round table. On the wall facing me
hangs a photograph of Abraham Lincoln and another of a figure so
mysterious and appealing that both Eric and I ask who it is.

"Corot," replies Alice, adding with a smile that one visitor mistook
it for Eleanor Roosevelt.

The prints and engravings that decorate the kitchen have the look
of illustrations from old chapbooks and remind me of my favorite pages
in the Provensens' *Mother Goose Book*. On the icebox hang notices,
reminders, and a little tin cake mold that, if put to use, would produce
an ornamental heart. A blue-willow tray on the sink and a bowl of
fruit are as lovely and complete as a still life.

"It's a good house for us," says Alice. "No huge drafty halls—
and just one of everything. One dining room, one kitchen, one library."

The library, which we visit after lunch, holds some of the handsome
and rare books that Alice has bound, including a three-volume edition
of Leonardo da Vinci's notebooks. I find myself especially drawn to a
book on falconry; the hunted beasts move from page to page on a

single line, like notes on a staff of ancient music. When I tell Martin that it reminds me of *A Peaceable Kingdom,* the Shaker abecedarius he and Alice illustrated, he smiles.

"We studied this book," he says.

Alice and Eric walk out to the barn to look at the studio; Eric has brought his camera and hopes to photograph there. Martin and I sit down at the kitchen table and talk.

Nancy Willard: Martin, what are some of the first books you remember?

Martin Provensen: The first books I remember were those my grandmother had on her farm in Iowa. She had the Doré Bible and *Pilgrim's Progress* and *Don Quixote*. So I was raised on some extraordinarily remarkable books. As for books written for children, there was *Alice in Wonderland,* of course. And then a series of books passed through my hands, most of the illustrators of which I've forgotten. But I do remember a book called *The Poppy Seed Cakes*.

NW: I loved that book too.

MP: When I was older, a group of books that meant a lot to me—and I still admire them—were the animal stories illustrated by Charles Livingston Bull. He drew animals very realistically, brilliantly, with a great deal of knowledge and skill. I think he worked in the late twenties and early thirties. When I was slightly older, I discovered Rackham and Dulac. And there was Kay Nielsen, who illustrated Danish fairy tales and whom I got to know at Disney Studios many years later. He was a great illustrator. All these books were very important to me.

NW: When did you go to work at Disney Studios?

MP: After I'd gone to Berkeley and UCLA, I went to Disney for one summer—this was in 1936—and I took a job for seventeen dollars a week. Not so bad in those days. I didn't like it very much, and they didn't like me either. I was fired. I then went over to a place called Harmon-Ising [a company of Hugh Harmon and Rudy Ising's, early animation producers] for six or seven months. They folded after I arrived. But I made several very good friends there, and when they went to the Disney Studio, they took me with them as excess baggage. I was lucky; when I'd first worked there, I was in the animation department, which I never would have liked. Although animation is the core of the studio and it's terribly important in making animated film, it didn't interest me that much. Animation is extraordinarily difficult and tedious—wonderful really, but it just didn't suit me. So I went into the story department, which I did like.

NW: I believe that kind of work has trained a good many illustrators.

MP: It was ideal training for book illustrating. Year after year we would sit together in a sort of assembly line to do storyboards, which were really walls of drawings. There were two or three of us in the group; I still keep in touch with two of my very best friends there, Aurelius Battaglia and John Miller, both well-known children's book illustrators. It was great training because we'd be given a sequence, the barest outline, just a thread of narrative, and then it was up to us to improvise on this theme. That was delightful; you could take it and play with it, and I must say this for Disney, he spared no expense. There was never a question of time; never "Let's get going with it, fellas." You could take months and months and at the end simply say, "No, we're not interested in this approach. Let's try something else." There were people around who had never seen a single drawing of theirs ever go into production. It didn't matter in those days. Disney created an atmosphere of experimentation, and what value came out of that studio was due to his willingness to take endless pains. Out of it, of course, came some of the best work the studio ever did: *Snow White*, *Pinocchio*, *Fantasia*.

NW: I can see, especially in the books about Maple Hill Farm, that some of the pages are organized like a sequence on film. A series of frames.

MP: When Alice was working in the film business, she started out as an animator. So she had the animation experience I didn't have, which we certainly use in our books—that concept of sequence and time, which is the essence of filmmaking.

NW: And of picture books.

MP: Yes—pursuing a concept through time. Have you ever seen Wilhelm Busch's drawings? He was one of the great German masters of the narrative cartoon. He would take an idea—say, a little boy walking down the road finds a package of flypaper. The situation builds and builds, often in a specifically scatological way, winding up bizarre. I won't go into it, but you can imagine what he could do with flypaper. We used Busch as a bible at Disney because of his inventiveness. He would take a concept and simply exhaust every possibility. He was remarkable.

NW: In *A Horse and a Hound, a Goat and a Gander*, you have one page that shows John the dog running to the right of the page at the top, then to the left just below it, and finally, at the bottom he finds the little girl hiding in the grass. Three images of the same subject in a single illustration. A favorite medieval Italian painting of mine, *The Meeting of Saint Anthony the Abbot With Saint Paul the Hermit,* does something very similar. The artist paints a single landscape and a road running over the mountain. In the top left-hand corner of the picture you see Saint Anthony walking along the road. To the right, farther down, he meets a centaur and resists his wiles. Then at the bottom of the picture, he embraces Saint Paul, and there is a wonderful entanglement of halos. It's the same concept of showing time in space, isn't it?

MP: You're probably right. There's no way to beat that way of telling a story—short of going into film. As long as you're committed to static drawings on a page, or a double spread, you simply can't improve that concept. We try to do the same thing. I'm glad you understood our picture of the dog the way you did. It's funny, but some editors, I am sorry to say, will look at a page like that and say, "Well, who are all these people?" They don't always follow the sequence because they're trained to see the unity of the single illustration. They can't see it as first one situation and then a new one on the same page. Occasionally you are confronted with people who can't be made to understand that the illustration is to be seen in time. You have to do it on page after page or break it up so clearly that they can't miss it.

NW: So many of your books deal with time, with the seasons, and you find so many different ways of showing time other than the obvious one—just turning the page.

MP: The fact that both Alice and I worked in film for years may be more important to us than we realize. I should also add that we both love the great Oriental scrolls. As you wind the scroll, you watch episode after episode. Such an enchanting change from turning the pages of a book.

NW: So the story really is continuous. The way life is.

MP: Yes, we've always longed at least to hint at that in a book. We try to capture as much of that as possible. We've not yet done it to our own satisfaction. We're still trying to find a way.

NW: In *A Peaceable Kingdom* you use the line for continuity.

MP: Yes, we do. Pull is terribly important in a book. If you don't capture the reader and make him want to turn the page and see what comes next, you've lost him before you've begun.

NW: What interests me about that book—and *A Visit to William Blake's Inn*—is this: How can you make a book look authentic and not pedantic? I know a lot of research went into these books, but they never look labored over.

MP: I suppose when a book works well, the material isn't something one has rushed to the library and done a lot of research about. In our case when a book works well, it's because we're using material that we've loved or been attracted to for a great many years. So we start out with some concept that is usually quite strong, and what we really have to do is check nuance and detail. It isn't as if one starts from scratch. We make a rough outline of the book.

With *William Blake's Inn,* for example, we know how many people love England and especially London, even if they haven't been there. Perhaps they carry an image in their heads based on all those Cruikshank drawings. When we were in London the year before, we wandered around a good deal, and though there isn't much left of eighteenth-century London, there is a bit here and there. The city has transcended its own destruction in a remarkable way; it still feels like an old city. Of course, there are a lot of other English cities that were not destroyed during the war and probably look a good deal as London looked in Blake's time. For example, Bath, a very elegant city. Both of us felt that from a town like Bath we could get an image of early London. And then you improvise. You don't have to be rigid about it.

NW: How do you and Alice work together on a book?

MP: Well, I like to remind everyone who asks us this question that books, throughout their history, were often illustrated by a group of people. You know the magnificent *Book of Hours* commissioned by the Duc de Berry. It's in Chantilly. Have you ever seen it?

NW: Not the original.

MP: Well, go to Chantilly someday. It's right there. A page is turned with a stick every week. So if you stay around long enough, you'll get to see the whole book. It's one of those great masterpieces of Western art, and it was done by the brothers de Limbourg. The de Limbourgs did about three-quarters of the book before they died, and another artist finished it. The point is, there was a collaboration.

Another enthusiasm of ours is the great Persian manuscripts, and as far as I can gather from reading, they were almost invariably worked on by groups of artists. One artist did the calligraphy, which was of course enormously important—perhaps more important than the pictures—another artist did the backgrounds, another did the animals, and so on. Perhaps not every book was done exactly in this way, but it was the usual method of illumination.

NW: That reminds me of the artists who made the cathedrals in Europe. We don't know who made the individual angels and beasts on the facades, and I don't think the artists cared that their names wouldn't be known.

MP: They didn't care at all. They knew between themselves who did what and they honored each other for their work. Theirs was a crafts-man's point of view.

NW: So your books are a collaboration in which you can't tell what you did and what Alice did?

MP: We don't worry about it. It's a matter of having confidence in your mutual understanding of what the goal is and how you want the book to look. I don't know how common this arrangement is now, but it's not something anyone invented today. The tradition has always been there.

NW: What goes into the design of a book?

MP: Well, the book is basically a vehicle for the text, so the text is the first thing. For the Blake book that we did together, Alice and I read your poems over a hundred times.

NW: You also read a lot of Blake's poetry, if I remember, and biog-raphies of Blake.

MP: We did read Blake, certainly. But when you begin a book, you read the text to get a sense of what it is, and then you think about the shape of the book—whether it should be vertical or horizontal— you think of the weight of the type, and the amount of type you should have on each page to balance the illustrations. Naturally, the younger the reader, the larger the print. Styles in typography change from year to year, just as styles in clothing change. If you look at the typefaces of the twenties and thirties, they will look very funny to you and old-fashioned. Sometimes they look nice, sometimes they don't, but you'll notice the flavor of an earlier time right away. There are even some designers who feel that book illustrations should only be in black and white because typography is black and white. This is a little rigid, I think.

NW: How would they deal with illuminated manuscripts?

MP: Well, they would answer that the capitals in illuminated manuscripts are colored, and therefore you can have colored capitals. On a logical basis, it's a hard thing to argue. I don't think you should be rigid about such things. In the first place, books today disappear with the speed of light, so that we're not dealing with an ultimate situation. Unfortunately, people often regard children's books as disposable.

NW: When do you hand-letter a text rather than have it set in type?

MP: We use hand lettering for capitals or titles when we want a stepping stone between the typography and the illustrations. For example, in *Myths and Legends* we hand-lettered the chapter headings. On jacket covers we often use hand lettering. Alice has a great feeling for this sort of work. So the physical character of books is very important to us. You have to start with the fact that the book is a *thing*. And yet it isn't a thing, because if you look at a book at midnight with no lights on, you turn this object over in your hands and what is it? It is as mysterious as a bat, it is a peculiar object that you can't really describe at all.

NW: Comparing books to bats—that delights me! In your books you are never very far from animals. Did you grow up with a lot of animals?

MP: No, not really, but both Alice and I love animals. Most children adore animals, and some adults never outgrow this passion. I think we fit into that category, as you can see by the way we live.

NW: When did you move to Maple Hill Farm?

MP: Thirty years ago.

NW: Where did you live before that?

MP: In Manhattan, on Fifty-seventh Street and Sixth Avenue, which we loved too. We still love New York, and we go in as often as we can afford to. We left Manhattan because our apartment building— the Sherwood Arms, a six-story brick studio building from the nineties—was being torn down. The rooms had fourteen-foot ceilings; they were marvelous. And we knew we'd never match it, never find a place like that again.

So we moved to Brooklyn Heights for a year. We were in the Margaret Hotel and had half of Joseph Pennell's studio. He was quite a well-known pen-and-ink artist and an etcher who did a great many industrial subjects in the twenties. The view of the harbor from that studio was incomparable, just magnificent. We always wanted to do a book about what we could see out of our window. I'm afraid we did very little work there because all day long we'd sit and look out at the city and the Statue of Liberty and the ships. The ships would come right in and dock at our feet.

NW: It would seem, though, that you have been able to draw and write about much that you have seen and known here at Maple Hill Farm. Are all the animals in your books animals you've lived with here?

MP: Yes. Almost all. Over thirty years, we've had a lot of animals because they live so short a span. We've never had cows; we brought in cows from the neighbors. That's poetic license. But we have had most of the others.

NW: I've always loved the names of the animals in your books: Evil Murdoch, Potato, Eggnog, Willow.

MP: Karen, our daughter, named a lot of the animals. She didn't intend them to be cute. She chose those names because that's the way the animals struck her. And we recognized the names as right, so we kept them. She still names most of our animals.

NW: Have you any favorite animals? Animals that you especially like to draw? I notice that you put a great many cats into your books.

MP: Well, I suppose we do have favorites, but all animals are fascinating to us. We'd like to have all sorts of animals if we could. You know, we just did a book about an owl that we had for a year. The more you relate to animals and the more you're around them, the more you develop a love for them. Animals are—for me and I think for Alice too—guides to the unknown. And what guides they are! Wasn't it Einstein who said that the mysterious is the most wonderful thing a human being can know?

I profoundly believe this. Einstein goes on to say that the mysterious is the basis of all art and all science and certainly all religion. I believe everything that makes life truly enchanting grows out of the quality of mystery. And I feel that animals are not simply cute and adorable but much more than that. For example, we have a cat who is maddening because she brings us corpses of animals. She kills and deposits the creatures here in the kitchen. I just spent the morning scraping guts off the floor in here, and I didn't particularly enjoy it. But this is an aspect of the animal that you can't deny or change. The cat doesn't understand that we don't enjoy her offerings.

NW: Was it you who told me once that cats bring their masters these offerings because they are trying to teach us how to hunt?

MP: What else? Certainly these offerings are gifts too. Dogs and cats form strong bonds with people. And lots of animals can be imprinted, as you know, so that they regard people as their parents. Ducks, for example. But certain dogs and cats form extraordinary attachments to people.

NW: What especially interests me in your drawings of cats is how often they are shown looking out of the drawing at the reader. I could only find one cat in your Mother Goose book that was seen in profile. The cats in your illustrations have such presence.

MP: Well, they are fascinating and alluring beings.

NW: You devote a couple of pages in *The Year at Maple Hill Farm* to the problems of getting animals to take medicine. And in *A Horse and a Hound, a Goat and a Gander* isn't there a picture of Evil Murdoch at the veterinarian's?

MP: We went through it all. You can't make that stuff up. I remember something that I don't believe we have in any of our books. A very good friend of ours, a neighbor in Sag Harbor, came up to visit us. When he arrived I was bathing a sick rooster's foot. The rooster was standing very quietly with one leg in the pail of solution while I bathed the foot. And our friend was astonished! He didn't know if it was a religious rite or what.

NW: Did you once tell me about a horse that came down with some sort of foot disease and required a similar treatment? And Alice read to you—

MP: She read a whole book about life in China while I applied compresses at four-hour intervals to the horse's leg. As you know, the circulation is poor in a horse's legs, so treatment had to be done almost constantly. He survived, though, so it worked.

NW: It's like helping a member of the family.

MP: I would hate to think that we are overly sentimental in our relationships with animals. We do recognize that animals are animals, and we find their presence rewarding. We also recognize that some people don't. Alice and I have friends who don't care about animals at all. Animals exist for them as food or as something useful—for pulling a wagon, perhaps. Well, I don't criticize them for that. But I do think animals have a great deal to teach people.

The barn holds the Provensens' studio, guest room, and henhouse—entered by a ramp on which Martin has nailed rungs for the convenience of small tenants. In the studio, light from the skylight touches a model Piper Cub on the worktable and some sketches of animals made in preparation for the books about Maple Hill Farm. I lift several sketches to look at a finished illustration done in oils on heavy board.

"Did you use oils for the illustrations in *William Blake's Inn?*"

"No," replies Martin, "those were done with acrylics."

And now my glance has fallen on a little shadow box, elegant and cunning as a marionette theater. On a checkered floor, minutely painted and flanked on two sides with mirrors to give the sense of infinite space, stands Harlequin.

"I saw an old box like this in Venice years ago," says Martin. "I'm in the process of making this one now."

A turn of the crank—and Harlequin's head vanishes. Another turn—and Harlequin is back again.

"Oh, tell me how it's done!"

"Never," says Martin with a laugh. "You think about it a little, though, and I'm sure you can figure it out. I'm crazy about toys just as you are."

On the table beside the shadow box is a tiny scroll in its own case. I bend over and crank it, and the lighter moments of the Provensens' trip to Paris unroll before me in a series of lively sketches. Before I reach the end of the trip, Eric enters the studio with his camera.

Alice and Martin seat themselves in front of the barn, and a great shaggy dog, whom I recognize as Muffin from *Our Friends at Maple Hill Farm,* bounds over to them just as Eric snaps the picture.

"The *Preppy Handbook* says you should call your daughter Muffin, not your dog," says Alice. "I'm glad we didn't read it before we got the dog."

"And you could call your daughter Spot," suggests Martin.

In this place of harmony between humans and beasts, I half expect Muffin to join the conversation.

"You must feel lucky being able to live here," says Eric.

"We do feel lucky," says Martin quietly, "lucky to live here, and lucky to really love what we're doing."

TELLING TIME

• • • • • • • • •

Once upon a time I received an advertisement in the mail for the complete stories of Chekhov, translated by Constance Garnett. The advertisement informed me that I would receive the first volume free—to get me hooked—and one volume every three months for three years, at the end of which I would own the complete Chekhov. More than seven hundred stories.

Seven hundred stories! I thought. Chekhov was a doctor. Any writer juggling the demands of a job, a novel in progress, and a family will probably ask, How did he find the time to write seven hundred stories? After I asked the question, I realized that how Chekhov found time for writing was less important to me than how I could find it.

Looking for answers, I began to keep track of how I spent my time as a writer.

September 4

I took out my notes for a new story. Mostly notes on characters. I feel as nervous starting out as if I were going to a party where I wouldn't know anybody. Will I like these characters? Will they like me? Will they tell me their secrets?

I could make an outline of the story I want to tell, but my characters don't like outlines. If I let them unfold in the writing itself, they'll reveal themselves in more interesting ways than my outline could ever have imagined for them. Getting to know your characters is like throwing a block party; you start with a few people, and suddenly the whole neighborhood shows up.

I've started the story with a conversation between the two main characters, by way of introducing them.

September 10

Today I met with my old friend and former editor at Harcourt Brace Jovanovich, Barbara Lucas, to discuss *Firebrat,* a fantasy novel I've almost finished. It was inspired by a painting of David Weisner's in which a boy and a girl emerge from the New York subway to find themselves in a kingdom where fish swim through the air and houses grow on trees. The character I call the Firebrat has nothing to do with David's painting. He's a six-foot scorpion and as pleasant as poison ivy.

Barbara liked the fantasy sections of the book but felt the scenes in the subway were vague. When my writing is vague, it's because I don't know enough about my subject. I need more concrete details. She also felt the character of the magician needed more work.

"What does he look like?" she asked. "All you've given your reader is dialogue."

I'm determined to spend an entire day riding the New York subway.

September 16

Dinner last night with Alice and Martin Provensen. Throughout the meal a golden retriever sat by Martin's chair and rested its head on his knee—the very image of canine devotion. The Provensens' farm is my idea of what the peaceable kingdom looks like: horses in a field, a boisterous rooster, any number of cats, a tribe of hens whom Martin has nicknamed the Thurbers, and a crotchety goose named Evil Murdoch. Martin told us that one fine fall day when the wild geese were flying and calling high overhead, Evil Murdoch was seen walking down the turnpike headed south.

At dinner we talked about plans for their daughter Karen's wedding, we talked about the naming of animals, we talked about everything except the one subject I was dying to bring up: the illustrations for the new book we're doing together, *The Voyage of the Ludgate Hill.* Though I'd love to see some sketches, Alice and Martin are as secretive as alchemists about what they're working on, especially toward the author. "If you showed in your face that you didn't like what we were doing, we would find it hard to go back to the drawing board in the same spirit we left it," Martin told me once.

It seems ages ago that they sent me a small volume of Robert Louis Stevenson's letters, asking if I could write a poem for them to illustrate based on a letter he wrote to Henry James in 1887. In that letter, Stevenson describes his voyage from London to New York on the good ship *Ludgate Hill:*

> I . . . enjoyed myself more than I could have hoped on
> board our strange floating menagerie: stallions and monkeys
> and matches made up our cargo; and the vast continent of
> these incongruities rolled the while like a haystack; and the
> stallions stood hypnotised by the motion, looking through
> the ports at our dinner-table, and winked when the crock-
> ery was broken; and the little monkeys stared at each other
> in their cages . . . ; and the big monkey, Jacko, scoured
> about the ship and rested willingly in my arms, to the ruin
> of my clothing . . . and the other passengers, where they
> were not sick, looked on and laughed. Take all this picture,
> and make it roll till the bell shall sound unexpected notes
> and the fittings shall break loose in our state-room, and you
> have the voyage of the *Ludgate Hill.*[1]

September 25

   While browsing in a secondhand shop, I came across a garden magazine intended for an audience of gardeners richer than I. Such wonderful articles telling you how to landscape your fifty acres with fountains, walls, terraces, etc. In the middle of an article on the Hellbrun palace in Salzburg, something took hold of me, some odd twist of association, and I heard one of my characters talking to herself. The most important thing for me, at this stage, is to get the voice right. The voice of whoever is telling the story.

   I haven't a clue as to how my story will end. But that's all right. When you set out on a journey and night covers the road, you don't conclude that the road has vanished. And how else could we discover the stars?

October 1

I spent the afternoon riding the New York subway. The train did not break down, an army of muggers did not set upon me with sticks, a fat man did not step on my feet, I did not get stuck in the turnstile, and the hole in my pocket did not send dimes and nickels and subway tokens spinning to the pavement.

This isn't to say that nothing happened. I have always liked Rilke's description of what happens when nothing is happening:

Who can name you all, you confederates of inspiration, you who are no more than sounds or bells that cease, or wonderfully new bird-voices in the neglected woods, or shining light thrown by an opening window out into the hovering morning; or cascading water; or air; or glances. Chance glances of passers-by. . . . Behold: they beckon here, and the divine line passes over them into the eternal.[2]

I came away with nothing so grand as a divine line passing over into the eternal, but I did meet an itinerant singer who was so like my idea of the magician in *Firebrat* that I almost thought I'd conjured him up. A starfish in his lapel, a mustache like the tusks of a walrus, fingers agleam with rings as he picked out "The Golden Vanity" on his guitar.

When I set about rewriting the subway scene in my manuscript, I knew what was missing. I'd mentioned the roar of the subway but not the silence and not the far-off drip drip drip of water seeping through the walls. I'd shown the jumble of graffiti on the cars but not the bleak space across the empty platforms after the train has left.

The magician in this book will look like the itinerant subway singer.

October 10

I sent *Firebrat* to my agent, who called to say she will submit it to Random House.

Back to my story. Worked on it last night and dreamed over it this morning. That twilight state between dreaming and waking is a good time for watching the story work itself out. I say *watching* because it really is like watching an animal, tracking it, understanding it, and finally training it.

By the harsh light of day I reread the two pages of conversation that open the story. Now they seem to me as clumsy as the opening scene in one of those melodramas in which the maid and the butler meet in the living room and discuss all the circumstances that have led up to the present crisis. The master has been away, the mistress is ill, the mistress's brother has gambled away the family fortune, etc. Naturally you never meet the maid and the butler again. Why should you? They're not characters. They're mouthpieces for conveying information.

I spent the morning groping for a way of dramatizing the information my reader will need to get on with my story. Well, I'm not writing a newspaper article. I don't need to give all the particulars of who, what, when, and where in the first paragraph. Isn't knowing when to withhold information one of the hard-won secrets of writing fiction? Did Stephen Crane worry about giving information when he wrote the opening sentence of "The Open Boat"?

"Nobody knew the color of the sky."

I want my opening sentence to let the reader know, as unobtrusively as possible, what kind of story he or she is spending time with. Realistic?

Fantasy? When D. H. Lawrence opens a story with "There was a man who loved islands. He was born on one, but it didn't suit him, as there were too many other people on it, besides himself",[3] I know right away that I'm in the presence of an extended parable.

October 14

A new building is going up in our neighborhood. The sign in front gives it a working title: Future Home of Zimmer Brothers' Jewelry Store. Since I pass it every morning on my way to buy the paper, I've seen the foundation poured, the girders laid, the walls rising. At this stage it looks like an empty swimming pool. Early one morning, before the regular crew had arrived, I saw a man standing at the bottom, all alone, unrolling a scroll. He was dressed like a workman with one curious exception: Instead of a yellow hard hat, he wore a visored cap with silver wings, and his glance rested on empty space as if he were about to perform a miracle. Building Rome in a day.

Two days later a drawing board stood on that very spot. On the drawing board lay the plans for the miracle. I felt as if I were looking at a gigantic metaphor for the way writers construct stories.

I've studied the plans for my story—they're all over my desk— but I haven't seen a man in a winged cap at the heart of it all. But I'm hoping for one—or maybe a winged lady, a sort of Winged Victory—who can convert my rough draft into a miracle.

Several years ago I read an article by Gail Godwin in which she suggested that having a mental picture of one's muse is very useful for overcoming writer's block. I tried it and discovered I had not one muse but two. Two sisters, one obsessively shy and the other obsessively tidy. The shy one was unavailable; she was always off walking in the woods. But the tidy one told me about her. Said she likes to sit under a certain pine tree looking for bones. An owl who lives in the tree eats dozens of mice every night, and every night he throws their bones away. A mouse's bones are no bigger than the gears in a watch. The shy sister makes whistles of them, so they'll sing when she breathes through them. The tidy sister is not fond of bones. The forest is her living room, and she can't bear to have mouse bones in her living room. She cleans and prunes and edits. Sometimes I want one sister, sometimes the other. But if I have writer's block, I know it's because the tidy sister is scolding the trees for growing and the milkweed for blowing, and then I hang out a sign for her: *Dear Madam: I Appreciate Your Services but Please Do Not Come Till You Are Called.* I can't have her around in the beginning when my poem or story is feeling its way into leaf and flower.

Finished three pages on my story. It's about a woman whose husband keeps changing jobs. Her great desire is to live in one place long enough to put down roots.

October 16

A day of distractions. The cat has an abscessed tooth; the cold-water faucet is broken in the bathroom; the light doesn't work in the cellar; and I've spent the morning on the telephone, pleading with plumbers and electricians. When I look at my manuscript, I feel I've lost the thread of the narrative. I have to resist the temptation to pile up page after page, to prove to myself that I am indeed writing. When I stop and ask myself, What is the story? I can't give myself a straight answer.

There's only one cure: to put the story on the back burner and turn to something else. I've always wanted to write a poem on our local hardware store—it's such a paragon of order and completeness.

Bins of nails, screws, latches for every purpose under heaven. Would that there were such a store for writers. Bins of opening lines, transitions, closing sentences—it would just be a matter of finding the one that fit.

When I tried to start the poem, I discovered I didn't even know the names of half the things I'd been seeing for years. I spent the afternoon at the hardware store, looking and learning. A careful examination of the commonplace is, for me, one of the best ways of keeping in touch with the man in the winged cap—or the shy sister in the forest.

October 18

Maria Modugno, my editor at Harcourt Brace Jovanovich, called to say that she is coming east. She'll stop at Alice and Martin's, pick up the illustrations for *Ludgate Hill,* and stay the night in Poughkeepsie with us.

October 20

My husband, Eric, told me a curious anecdote about an electrical engineer he knows at work who is taking early retirement so that he can devote full time to his writing. He came to writing many years ago with no background in literature at all. "All my life," he told Eric, "I saw the world so differently from the way my friends saw it that I figured I must be a little crazy." The difference had something to do with imagination and intuition, though at the time he didn't use those words to explain it.

One day he picked up a copy of the *New Yorker* in a doctor's office and read the first story. If I'm crazy, he told himself, the guy who wrote this story is crazy in the same way I am.

He read the next story and the next with growing excitement, and on the way home from the doctor's office he mailed his subscription card to the *New Yorker* and eagerly awaited the first issue. He read every issue from cover to cover, and one day he sat down to write a story of his own.

The writing went smoothly enough, but having finished his story, he did not know how to submit it. So he called the *New Yorker* to find out. The receptionist was amused and patient.

"You put the story in an envelope," she explained, "and you include return postage. And then you wait for an answer."

He waited. He waited for six months. He waited the way we have all waited. After six months, he called the magazine. The kind receptionist told him a letter was in the mail. Two days later he received the letter. The *New Yorker* wanted to buy his story. He was ecstatic. How many people sell their first story to the *New Yorker*?

But his second and third stories did not fare so well. They came back bearing notes from Rachel MacKenzie, an editor known for her candor: "This stinks."

I can't help thinking of what a friend of mine said when I congratulated him on the acceptance of his first novel. "Now I'm trying to start the second one. I thought it would be easier. Well, it's not. I'm right back in square one."

October 28

Maria Modugno, my editor at HBJ, arrived yesterday evening, and we arranged the artwork for *Ludgate Hill* in the living room on the sofa and along the walls, and then we ooh'd and ah'd. She told me that when she arrived at their studio, Alice and Martin were frowning at the page on which a lively baboon makes its first appearance.

"It needs a little more blue," said Alice.

Martin picked up his brush and added a single stroke. Turning to Maria, Alice gave Martin a compliment that came from forty-two years of being happily married and making fifty-six books together.

"Nobody paints baboons better than Martin," said Alice.

Maria spent the night on our living-room sofa. At midnight a huge raccoon tried to batter his way through the cat door. At two in the morning the cat himself began playing the piano by walking up and down on the keys. I fear she will never accept our hospitality again.

I finished the poem on the hardware store.

A HARDWARE STORE AS PROOF
OF THE EXISTENCE OF GOD

I praise the brightness of hammers pointing east
like the steel woodpeckers of the future,
and dozens of hinges opening brass wings,
and six new rakes shyly fanning their toes,
and bins of hooks glittering into bees,

and a rack of wrenches like the long bones of horses,
and mailboxes sowing rows of silver chapels,
and a company of plungers waiting for God
to claim their thin legs and walk away laughing.

In a world not perfect but not bad either
let there be glue, glaze, gum, and grabs,
calk also, and hooks, shackles, cables, and slips,
and signs so spare a child may read them,
Men, Women, In, Out, No Parking, Beware the Dog.

In the right hands, they can work wonders.[4]

November 1

Something there is that doesn't love a word, and it took up residence in the word processor I'm learning—with difficulty—to use. I had got all the way up to page nineteen of my story when the screen flashed a message: Disk Error. Sentences slid into gibberish; words collapsed into cuneiform. The last line I'd written began pulsing like a mad neon sign. I exited, as the expression goes, turned off the machine, and fled downstairs to make a cup of coffee. When I returned to my story half an hour later, all but three lines were gone.

Immediately I put in a new disk and wrote out as much as I could remember of what I'd lost. A few hours later, I sat down at the PC and summoned up my hastily written memories of those lost pages. Gone. I'm unspeakably depressed.

November 2

I rose at dawn and wrote out my story for the third time, and for the third time it vanished. Eric and I spent the day trying to diagnose the problem. If machines were murderable, this one would be dead. I've gone back to the 1936 Smith-Corona that I bought for twenty-four dollars in a secondhand shop. Like a faithful family retainer, it runs without complaint. Naturally I'm forced to write more slowly. But this has its advantages. When you write slowly, you give the odd associations that hang around the edges of a scene their due. It's like zipping through the countryside in a limousine that suddenly breaks down. I have to get out and walk, and that's when I discover the chicory, the wild grapevine, and the ten different species of wild grasses.

To write fast enough and at the same time to write slowly

enough—isn't that the paradox at the heart of the writer's dilem-ma about finding time? This afternoon when I was in the library, the title of an article in the *Writer's Digest* caught my eye: "How to Write Fast." I picked up the magazine and leafed through it and found myself diverted by a list of books deemed useful for writers: *Writing the Novel: From Plot to Print; How to Write While You Sleep . . . and Other Surprising Ways to Increase Your Writing Power; How to Stop Snoring; Make Your House Do the Housework; How to Find Another Husband . . . By Some-one Who Did; Writing After Fifty; Waking Up Dry: How to End Bedwetting Forever.*

You could buy a laminated walnut writer's block if you sent fifteen dollars to the right party. A sort of voodoo item, I guess; you could pass it on to the writer who gives you a bad review.

I suppose we all want to write faster. At our backs we hear time's winged chariot, and when we try to set ourselves schedules for writ-ing, it's because writing is work, and nobody can do this work for us.

But finding time isn't enough. It must be the right kind of time, and the right kind of time is as hard to find as truffles or wild orchids. The time by which the man in the winged cap and the shy sister in the forest live—that's the kind I want. And that kind of time knows nothing about schedules. It's close to what one scholar of Native American art has described as the Indian sense of time:

> It teaches the great lesson of patience, and in this it com-mands respect. . . . Although Indians say nothing about it, the artistic part of their culture is . . . created in the frame-work of ceremonial time—slow time. . . . Pueblo clay can only be gathered when conditions are right and after pray-ers are said. . . . While creating, they are inside time and

react to an internal rhythm that cannot be talked about, but which is nevertheless there. Ceremonial time is private time. Many craft workers do not like to be observed while working, and the firing of Pueblo pottery is mostly done in secret.[5]

November 4

My agent called to say that Random House wants to buy *Firebrat*. Janet Schulman, the editor, wants numerous revisions, and she has offered to come to Poughkeepsie so that we can discuss them. Oh, I hoped she'd think it was perfect. Sometimes I think all I want is to be praised.

I hate to interrupt the story I'm doing now to tinker with a book I let go of months ago. When a book is finished, the connection between me and the characters is broken. In a year or two I'll have forgotten their names. They become like the people you meet on a trip. You send them Christmas cards till you realize you can't recall what they look like.

November 23

A good friend has just been accepted for a three-week stint at the Virginia Colony of the Arts. Concentration, a gift of time: it does wonders for your writing, he assured me.

I suppose it does. But I'd miss the connection with everyday life —my son, James, coming home at three, telling tales out of school. Like the one about the science teacher who keeps dead mice in his freezer to feed his pet boa constrictor. One day when the snake looked particularly famished, he popped a frozen mouse into the microwave. A small gray explosion followed. There are no oven-cleaning compounds on the market guaranteed to banish entrails of mouse.

December 10

Today Janet Schulman came to Poughkeepsie, and we went over the manuscript of *Firebrat*. Right off she wanted me to change the title, and I felt like my immigrant relatives from Sweden who lost their good family name somewhere on Ellis Island. "Too many Martinsons here already," snapped an official. "From now on, your name is Hedlund."

It seems that Simon and Schuster is coming out with a series of young adult books called *The Firebrats,* about teenagers after a nuclear disaster.

"How about calling it *The Quest for Firebrat?*" suggested Janet.

Quest is a word I abhor. What if Lewis Carroll had called his book *Alice's Quest for Wonderland?* What if L. Frank Baum had called his *Dorothy's Quest for the Emerald City?* To me, *quest* suggests a pale imitation of King Arthur, a pasteboard medieval story.

So my title will have to stay.

Her other suggestions were fine. The skill of a good editor never fails to amaze me—that perfect blend of severity and understanding. Janet reminds me of pleasant-faced Mrs. Bowman, who worked in the AAA office in Ann Arbor. Every summer when I was in high school our family drove from Ann Arbor, Michigan, to Albuquerque, New Mexico, where my father was teaching summer school. A week before the trip, he'd sit down with Mrs. Bowman, and with much folding and refolding of maps, they would discuss the dangers and possibilities. The cities where it was easy to get lost. The towns where you could see notable attractions. My father did not care for museums, but he was never in such a hurry that he wouldn't stop to see something advertised—usually on a hand-lettered sign in the middle of the desert—as a notable attraction. The crater left by a falling star. The rattlesnake that killed the mayor's wife in a town so small you could blink twice and miss it altogether. Never mind that the notable attractions we saw were notable to nobody else. When he left the AAA office, he carried a book of strip maps with our route carefully marked in red.

Years later, sitting in on one of John Gardner's workshops at the Bread Loaf Writers' Conference, I thought of those strip maps. John was telling how he kept track of details when he worked on a long novel. Shelf paper, he said. You unwind the roll. You tape it to the four walls of your room. You divide it into chapters, leaving plenty of space between them, because you'll soon be filling those spaces with notes. You could call it a map to help you navigate the unknown waters of your novel-in-progress. But never forget that you're in charge of the terrain. After all, you invented it. If that wonderful cleaning woman you so casually introduced in Chapter Three keeps trying to take over the story, you just might want to change the map.

Janet did have a few misgivings about the character of the magician. "Some of the details you use to describe him don't connect with anything else in the book," she remarked.

I started to tell her that it was all true, that I'd seen this wonderful itinerant singer in the subway. And then I stopped. Oh, I'd succumbed to one of the writer's strongest temptations: the wish to include something because it really happened.

December 27

Eric and James and I spent the Christmas holidays zipping between Ann Arbor and Grosse Pointe and Toledo, visiting our mothers and other relatives. Yesterday Eric and James returned home. I'm staying in Ann Arbor over the New Year to take care of Mother. She's had what the doctor calls a series of small strokes. Small to him, maybe, but not to her. At a single stroke she's lost some of her most precious memories, and hoping to find them again, she asks the same questions over and over: Did I have a wedding? Is my sister still alive? How did my mother die?

When darkness falls, a nameless anxiety overtakes her. Her doctor calls it the sundown syndrome. All night long she goes up and down the stairs, checking to see if the doors are locked, peeking into every room in the house. "Who's staying with me? Whose house is this?" she asks. "Am I alone? Did I sleep here last night?" She dreamed that somebody kidnapped her and held her for ransom.

Sleep is impossible for both of us. She sleeps so lightly. Every ten minutes she comes into my room and turns on the light on the pretext of bringing me something.

At two A.M. she lugged in a huge portrait of my grandfather. At three A.M. she was standing by my bed, holding her college diploma.

"Do you know where your diploma is?" she asked.

When she finally went to bed at four, I fell asleep and dreamed that all the cars in Ann Arbor had identical bumper stickers: It's three A.M. Do You Know Where Your Diploma Is?

December 30

After four nights of not getting to sleep before four in the morning I feel like a zombie. Sunday when I tried to wake Mother up for church, she threatened to call the Humane Society and report me. I was determined to get her out of the house. We made it to church in time for the closing benediction. Mother turned to me and said, "That's the shortest service I've ever heard in my life."

Border's bookshop was open. We stopped to browse. I bought Troyat's biography of Chekhov to read while Mother is roaming around the house at night. Last night around three A.M. she brought me some literature left by the Jehovah's Witnesses: a magazine called *Awake* and a book called *How to Get Into Paradise*.

December 31, 1986

New Year's Eve. We are watching old Cary Grant movies and the news and the weather. Over and over, the same news, the same weather.

I've started reading the Chekhov biography by the flickering light of the TV and feel humbled. The description of his life in Moscow during a typhus epidemic puts my sleepless nights into perspective.

> Like all doctors he was constantly on call, and he slept only a few hours a night. . . . Even when he could grab a bit of time from his patients, he had trouble concentrating on the blank page. An entire floor of the building where he lived was occupied by a caterer, who used it for wedding receptions, funeral dinners, and guild banquets, and the shouting, the blare of music, the tinkle of dishes never seemed to end. To Bilibin he wrote: "There is a wedding orchestra playing over my head at the moment. . . . Some asses are getting married and stomping away like horses"; and to Leikin: "I've been so exhausted, frenzied and crazed these past two weeks that my head is spinning . . . The flat is constantly full of people, noise, music. . . . The office is cold. . . . The patients keep coming.[6]

Who am I to complain about one ailing mother?

January 3, 1987

Last night I took the train back to Poughkeepsie. When I stepped up to the ticket window to ask when my train was leaving, I was clutching the Chekhov biography. The ticket taker looked at it and smiled.

"Chekhov! Hey, you a *Star Trek* fan?"

February 27

Tying up the newspapers for recycling, I fell to reading old Sunday magazine sections of the *New York Times*. How could I have missed the issue with the photograph of Joan Didion in her study in California? Her window faces the ocean, her desk is so vast she could tap-dance on it. A room of her own—full of purpose and space and light.

My study, which I share with my son, James, commands a fine view of Franklin's funeral parlor. On a busy day, they do as many as eight funerals over there. The mourners arrive, the hearses gather them up. When the last hearse has vanished, Mrs. Franklin runs outside and hangs up her laundry. When the next batch of mourners arrives, she takes it all down again. Sometimes at night an ambulance comes, its lights flashing.

It is nearly midnight. Eric is working in his darkroom, and in the next room James is reading a new Phil Dick novel. A repetitive tune—I think it's something from a tape of the Grateful Dead—drifts through the closed door. All this coming and going does sharpen one's sense of time. How it passes.

March 29

This afternoon—a warm Sunday, the daffodils are nodding, the tulips are sending up brilliant globes to light the shady beds of violets—this afternoon I got a call from a friend of Alice and Martin Provensen.

"I wanted to tell you this before you read it in the newspaper," she said. "Martin died of a heart attack on Friday morning."

I was so stunned that I hardly heard her account of how it happened. He'd stepped outside and raised his hand to hail the man who was picking up fallen brush. Was Martin greeting him? Calling for help? The next moment he collapsed.

Alice had gone into town on an errand, and she returned to see the ambulance pulling out of the road that leads to their farm. She rode with Martin to the hospital. I remembered Emily Dickinson: "Because I could not stop for Death, he kindly stopped for me." What else could she do but go along for the ride—at least as far as the border? When Chekhov lay dying of tuberculosis, the doctor ordered champagne for him instead of oxygen.

There will be no funeral and no memorial service. I think of Hans Christian Andersen's instructions to the friend who was composing a funeral march for him: "Most of the people who will walk after me will be children, so make the beat keep time with little steps."

Eric and James and I jumped into the car and drove to the Provensen farm. Friends had been dropping in all day. We sat around the table in the kitchen; the coffeepot was steaming, and everywhere we saw signs of Martin's life on earth. His cap and jacket hung on the hook by the door, his heart medicine stood on the kitchen shelf.

Their daughter, Karen, returned from the funeral parlor.

"I saw Dad," she said. "He was wearing his favorite red-checked shirt. I sat by the coffin and talked and talked. I'm so glad I could say good-bye."

Alice stood up. "I should go to the funeral parlor too!" she exclaimed.

Martin's best friend touched her arm. "No," he said. "You said good-bye to him in the ambulance. The real Martin isn't in the funeral parlor. You know he always said he didn't believe in the body."

For artists, for writers, what body is there but the body of work we leave behind?

March 30

I can't even imagine what it would be like to lose someone with whom you had done fifty-six books. Going to work every morning for Alice and Martin did not mean the separation that it does for so many couples: he leaves for one office, she for another. Day after day in the studio, the only voices they heard were each other's.

When I saw the obituary for Martin in the *New York Times,* I understood why we need poems. Facts tell us everything and nothing. I happened to mention this paradox to a gentleman who runs one of the two bookshops in our neighborhood, and he told me a story his Irish grandfather told him, a story that may be another way of saying the same thing. The god Lir created the world by speaking the names of everything in it. Because he had only half a tongue, his words were only half understood. Half of creation, therefore, remained unspoken. That's why we need poets: to sing the hidden side of things.

April 3

I've set my story aside to write an elegy for Martin. Chekhov, as always, has good advice: "When you . . . wish to move your readers to pity, try to be colder. It will give a kind of backdrop to . . . grief, make it stand out more. . . . Yes, be cold."[7]

Worked on the elegy. Literature from Bread Loaf is arriving. Oh, Chekhov would have enjoyed that place. He might have been talking about Bread Loaf and not the Crimea when he confessed to family and friends: "I haven't written a line. . . . I'm gradually turn-

ing into a talking machine. Now that we've solved all existing problems, we've started in on problems never raised before. We talk and
talk and talk; we may die of inflammation of the tongue and vocal
cords."[8]

Chekhov could have run a fine workshop, judging from the critiques
he gave to writers who sent him manuscripts. How did he find time
to answer them all?

> You have so many modifiers that the reader has a hard
> time determining what deserves his attention, and it tires
> him out. If I write, "A man sat down on the grass," it is
> understandable because it is clear. . . . But it would be hard
> to follow and brain-taxing were I to write, "A tall narrow-
> chested, red-bearded man of medium height sat down
> noiselessly, looking around timidly and in fright, on a patch
> of green grass that had been trampled by pedestrians." The
> brain can't grasp all that at once, and . . . fiction ought to
> be immediately . . . graspable.[9]

April 11
I finished the elegy for Martin.

LITTLE ELEGY
WITH BOOKS AND BEASTS

in memory of Martin Provensen (1916–1987)

I

Winters when the gosling froze to its nest
he'd warm it and carry it into the house praising

its finely engraved wings and ridiculous beak—
or sit all night by the roan mare, wrapping
her bruised leg, rinsing the cloths while his wife
read aloud from *Don Quixote,* and darkness hung
on the cold steam of her breath—
or spend five days laying a ladder for the hen
to walk dryshod into the barn.

Now the black cat broods on the porch.
Now the spotted hound meeting visitors, greets none.
Nestler, nurse, mender of wounded things,
he said he didn't believe in the body.
He lost the gander—elder of all their beasts
(not as wise as the cat but more beloved)—
the night of the first frost, the wild geese
calling—last seen waddling south
on the highway, beating his clipped wings.

II

He stepped outside through the usual door
and saw for the last time his bare maples
scrawling their cold script on the low hills
and the sycamore mottled as old stone
and the willows slurred into gold by the spring light,
and he noticed the boy clearing the dead brush—
old boughs that broke free under the cover of snow,
and he raised his hand, and a door in the air opened,
and what was left of him stumbled and fell
and lay at rest on the earth like a clay lamp

still warm whose flame was not nipped or blown
but lifted out by the one who lit it
and carried alive over the meadow—
that light by which we read, while he was here,
the chapter called Joy in the Book of Creation.[10]

April 13

As I trudged to the post office to mail the poem to the *New Yorker,* I remembered my favorite rejection letter. It was written by the editor of a Chinese journal and appeared in a London paper:

We have read your manuscript with boundless delight. If we were to publish your paper, it would be impossible for us to publish any work of a lower standard. And as it is unthinkable that in the next thousand years we shall see its equal, we are, to our regret, compelled to return your divine composition, and to beg you a thousand times to overlook our short sight and timidity.[11]

April 25

Worked on my story.

A call from Anatole Broyard at the *New York Times.* Would I review a book on Dvořák in America? The review should be eight hundred words.

Chekhov's advice to a young writer who felt pressured for time seems to be meant for me: "Stop trying to meet deadlines. I do not know what your income is: if it is small, then starve, as we starved in our youth, but keep your observations for works you . . . write during the blissful hours of inspiration, not in one go."[12]

Broyard described the book he wished to send me: *Spillville,* by

Patricia Hampl. A pilgrimage to the small town in Iowa where Dvořák spent a summer. The more he talked, the more interesting it sounded.

I thought of Chekhov. I asked myself, Do I have the time? I want to finish my story, and I'm going to be in Ann Arbor again at the end of May, taking care of my mother.

Because he told me I have the whole month of June to write it, I said yes.

May 22

The galleys I'm to review arrived—along with a fat book on Dvořák, which Broyard thought would help, and a note telling me the review is due June 3. Did I mishear the date or did he change it? I've started to work on it right away.

May 23

"There are two worlds, the post office and nature," wrote Thoreau in his journal (January 3, 1853). "I know them both."

Today I got a letter from a child who asked: "Are you famous? Are any of your books a movie yet?"

I wrote back and said no to both questions. But who knows what tomorrow's mail will bring? When Random House issued a new edition of *The History of Henry Esmond,* the editors received a letter from a Hollywood agent addressed to William Makepeace Thackeray. "In the event that you have already made a commitment to some agent for the above book, we nevertheless are impressed with your potential possibilities as a screen writer and would be interested in both your services and future stories." What a prime candidate for the dead-letter office.

Random House replied as follows: "Thank you for your letter. . . . I am now working on a new novel which I think will be a natural for pictures. I am thinking of calling the new book *Vanity Fair*."[13]

May 25

A fit of gardening has thrown my back out of kilter; I can't even climb out of bed. My review is due at the end of the week. Lying on my back, I tried to write, but the ink in my pen has no imagination and refuses to flow uphill. The bed is a stagnant sea of papers, books, and cats.

Oh, I should have taken Chekhov's advice.

May 26

"A man may write at any time," said Samuel Johnson, "if he will set himself doggedly to it."

I crept out of bed and found that by kneeling at the PC I could write a little. Anyone seeing me would have supposed I was praying for inspiration.

Rilke says kneeling is the right spiritual posture for an artist: "He who kneels, who gives himself wholly to kneeling, loses the measure of his surroundings. . . . He . . . belongs to that world in which height is—depth—and . . . who could measure the depth?"[14]

May 28

The review for the *Times* is done. Mailed it off this morning.

June 1

I'm in Ann Arbor taking care of Mother. On the way back from the train station, we stopped to visit the grave of her firstborn son, who died three hours after he was born. Years later, when I was growing up, she still talked about him, calculating his age, wondering what kind of person he'd have become.

"I heard him cry," she'd tell me. "I heard the doctor say he'd fit in a teacup. The nuns told me they'd baptized him."

Now he lies under a small headstone in the infant section of the cemetery, in the flock of stone lambs marking the surrounding graves. That boy I was born to replace. Today Mother looks at the grave without interest.

"I can't remember my wedding," she says suddenly. "Did I have a wedding?"

"You did," I say. "You were married at home. You had a luncheon afterward."

Silence.

"Was I a good mother? I can't remember."

"You were a wonderful mother," I say. "You still are."

"Wasn't I lucky to have you!" she says, beaming. "Think of all the daughters I could have had. My mother was wonderful too," she adds proudly. Pause. "She was so good at taking away pain."

I think of Emerson at seventy, stricken with what we now know was Alzheimer's, fighting his memory loss by sticking labels onto things, describing their use. The names meant nothing to him anymore. The sign on his umbrella read: The Thing That Strangers Take Away. So he spent the last years of his life living among riddles he made himself. At Longfellow's funeral he murmured to a friend, "That gentleman had a sweet, beautiful soul, but I have entirely forgotten his name."

Easy enough to riddle an umbrella. Not so easy to riddle a human life. The Sphinx asks, and Oedipus answers. What goes on four legs in the morning, two legs at noon, and three in the evening?

Last night, Mother was up till four, checking the doors and asking questions. Always the same questions. But sometimes, when the muse is with me, I hear them differently. I listen the way those Irish poets listened who wanted to speak for the dark side of creation.

I have gone to bed in my old room, which still has the luminous stars that my father pasted on the ceiling so many years ago. My mother stands in the hall, her shadow falling into my room, and the whole universe sparkles between us.

"Where are we?" she asks. "Who's with us? Where did we come from? Will we still be here tomorrow?"

NOTES

[1] Robert Louis Stevenson, *The Letters of Robert Louis Stevenson,* Sir Sidney Colvin, ed. (New York: Charles Scribner's Sons, 1925), 7.

[2] Rainer Maria Rilke, *Selected Works: Vol. I, Prose,* G. Craig Houston, trans. (Norfolk, Conn.: New Directions, 1960), 60–61.

[3] D. H. Lawrence, "The Man Who Loved Islands," *The Complete Short Stories,* Vol. III (London: William Heineman Ltd., 1961), 722.

[4] Nancy Willard, "A Hardware Store as Proof of the Existence of God," *Water Walker* (New York: Knopf, 1989), 16.

[5] Ralph T. Coe, *Lost and Found Traditions, Native American Art 1965–1985* (Seattle: University of Washington Press, in association with the American Federation of Arts, 1967), 31, 33, 34.

[6] Henry Troyat, *Chekhov,* Michael Henry Heim, trans. (New York: E. P. Dutton, 1986), 69–70.

[7] Ibid., 148.

[8] Ibid., 97.

[9] Ibid., 223.

[10] Nancy Willard, "Little Elegy with Books and Beasts," in *Water Walker* (New York: Alfred A. Knopf, 1989), 47.

[11] James Charlton and Lisbeth Mark, *The Writer's Home Companion* (New York: Franklin Watts, 1987), 28.

12 Troyat, 71.

13 Charlton and Mark, 66–67.

14 Rainer Maria Rilke, *Letters of Rainer Maria Rilke*, Vol. II, Jane Bannard Greene and Herten Norton, M.D., trans. (New York: W. W. Norton Company, Inc., 1948), 238–39.

CLOSE ENCOUNTERS

OF THE

STORY KIND

· · · · · · · · ·

Once upon a time an editor, knowing my fascination with angels, invited me to write a story about one, and I thought, Here's an assignment after my own heart, and I said yes. Then I panicked.

What did I know about angels?

The first angel I ever saw had a chipped nose. It was blond, male, and lived in a clock that hung in the parlor of the apartment Mrs. Lear rented in my grandmother's house in Owosso, Michigan. When the hour struck, two doors opened at the top and a tiny platform revolved, bearing the archangel Michael from one door to the next. Such dignity, such beauty. He was a procession of one. Mrs. Lear's husband had fought in the First World War and brought it from

Germany, along with a Luger and some empty shells. A local jeweler who repaired it told him that it must have once held other figures, probably Adam and Eve being driven from the garden. Time had taken the archangel's sword, the fugitives, and the tip of his holy nose. Nevertheless, when I knew the hour was preparing to strike, I would knock on Mrs. Lear's door and ask to see the angel moving from darkness into darkness. When the novelty wore off and I no longer asked, Mrs. Lear would knock on my grandmother's apartment to announce the angel was marching and did I want to watch it?

An angel marching from darkness into darkness—such an event should not go unnoticed.

The second angel I saw was a picture from an old insurance calendar that my grandmother had saved long after the year was out. A young woman in a white nightgown stood with arms outstretched over two children playing at the edge of a cliff. There was a large asterisk of apple butter on her wings, as if someone had hurled a full jar during an argument and the angel had taken a blow intended for someone else. The calendar hung in my grandfather's treatment room, where patients with rheumatism and asthma went to avail themselves of the wonders of osteopathy. Only the angel and our family knew that the treatment room had once been a pantry and the waiting room doubled as the doctor's bedroom; my grandfather unfolded the sofa at night to sleep in, and in the morning folded it up again before the office opened. Grandmother, who managed the renting of the other rooms, had her own quarters off the kitchen.

Though I have seen many images of angels since these two, they seem the real ones, the standard by which all others should be measured.

Two days after I'd agreed to write a book about angels, my sister, Kirsten, called from Ann Arbor with bad news.

"Mother fell and broke her hip," she said, "so I grabbed the first plane out of Pittsburgh last night. The doctor said he wants to give her a new one."

"A new hip? At eighty-seven?"

"He said it's her only chance of walking. And it's man-made, so it's even better than her old one. It will last forever."

"Is she conscious?"

"She's right here. I'll put her on the phone."

I pressed my ear to the receiver and heard nothing.

"Mother? How are you feeling?"

She did not answer for a long time, and when she did, she sounded far off, as if she were speaking from a different room.

"Isn't it the limit I should have to go through this?" she whispered.

A long silence, broken by Kirsten's voice. "I found Mother's purse. It's been missing for two months. And now we can't find her teeth. They've simply vanished for good and all."

"How long will she be in the hospital?"

"A week. They like to get you out early here. But we'll need round-the-clock care when she moves home."

"What about taking her to Shady Park?" I asked. "Can they keep her?"

From the house she'd lived in for fifty years my mother had moved to a single large room in Shady Park Manor, a convalescent home in Pittsburgh five blocks from my sister and her husband. She had a room of her own. Kirsten had made sure of that. On its bare surfaces my sister put spindles of snapshots; on its white walls she hung the brass filigree frames that kept us all in line: me in my cap and gown standing beside Daddy in the cap and gown he wore only when pressed into marching at commencement; my sister in her wedding dress, rising from a swirl of lace; the grandchildren, who had long ago outgrown their school portraits; Mother's diploma from Michigan, its blue-and-gold ribbon faded but intact. The bureau held her lavender underwear, her nylons, her purple shoes. The closet held all ten of her best purple dresses.

This was the room I saw when I arrived from New York. The classes I taught at Vassar were finished; Kirsten and John would be gone for two weeks. The note in the kitchen laid out my duties.

"Please take in the mail, water the plants in the dining room, and feed the tortoise. He only eats scraped carrots. Scraper is on sink. Please take Mother's dresses to the laundromat and wash them on *delicate*. They wash everything in hot water at the home."

Every morning I walked the five blocks to Shady Park, past the Fourth Presbyterian Church and the synagogue, past the Greek restaurant, the Cafe del Sol, the Korean grocer who hangs strings of jade beads in the window among the melons. Past Eat'n Park, where families carry heaping plates from the salad bar and single men sit at the counter, drinking coffee and smoking. Past Isaac's Vegetarian Deli and Tucker's Secondhand Books.

Shady Park Manor stands over all, at the top of a steep hill. I hurry through the lobby, beautifully decorated in silver-and-blue wallpaper, up the stairs, past the nurses' station. When I arrive at my mother's room, she is sitting up in her chair, asleep, belted in, like a passenger in a plane about to land. But somewhere deep in the body of the plane, the fatigued metal has given way and sent this one woman, still strapped to her seat, hurtling through space.

Over my mother's bed, someone has taped a list of instructions:

> 7:30: Get Mrs W. up to eat breakfast. Be sure dentures
> are in with Fast-Teeth powder.
> 8:00–2:00: Keep Mrs W. up once she is in chair. She will
> fight to go back to bed, but she needs to be kept active.

"Mom," I say, "wake up!"

She opens her eyes.

"What is this place?"

"A condominium," I lie. "Come on, Ma, let's get the wheelchair and go for a spin around the block."

"Why can't I walk? What's the matter with me?"

"You broke your hip."

I unfold the wheelchair and lift her into it. She is staring at my feet.

"You need new shoes," she says.

We both gaze down at my scuffed loafers. Miles of pavement have pared the heels away and loosened the stitching.

"Promise me you'll buy a new pair. Take some money from my purse. Where is my purse?"

I hand it to her. She opens it and peers in and twitches up a five-dollar bill.

"Didn't I have more money than this when I started?"

"Oh, Mother, you don't need any money here."

"Is this an old people's home?"

"It's a condominium, Ma."

"It's a home. I never thought my children would put me in a home."

"Ma, you need twenty-four-hour care."

"What did people do in the old days?"

What *did* they do? Dutiful daughters struggled with lifting, feeding, and changing their aged parents. I thought of my mother under the stress of caring for her own mother, who lived with us when I was growing up. Does my mother remember the night she got up to go to the bathroom and passed out from exhaustion? She landed against the radiator. Now, at the edge of her short sleeve I can see the long scar on my mother's arm, deep as a knife wound, where the flesh burned slowly away as she lay, numb to the pain. These dutiful women—"caregivers" is the current term for them—did not go off to jobs in the morning. And they certainly were not writers.

We pass the nurses' station and the board that lists the day's activities: talking book club, pet therapy, Monday night movie, Bingo, current events, sensory stimulation, this month's birthdays. In the all-purpose room, the physical therapist is tossing a beach ball to a group of men and women in wheelchairs. None of them raise their arms. As I wheel Mother outside into the sunshine, she raises a pleading face to mine.

"Can't you find a little corner in your house for me?"

In the evening, when I unlock the door of my sister's house the tortoise creeps out of his shell and crosses the kitchen floor to meet me. His ancient eyes blink while I scrape his carrots, letting the shavings pile up on the plate like golden pages. Outside in the shimmering heat, children play Hide and Seek and call to one another. The bedroom is suffocating. I carry my sheet and pillow downstairs and make a bed on the living-room floor. I read another chapter in John Gardner's *Art of Fiction* and underline a sentence that sounds like good advice—if only I knew how to follow it: " . . . fiction does its work by creating a dream in the reader's mind."[1] The last sound I hear before falling asleep is the tortoise taking his constitutional, the faint scraping of his claws along the floor.

Have I told you everything? No. I have not told you how every evening I sat down at my brother-in-law's electric portable and worked on my story. A story about an angel.

The hardest part of writing a story or a novel is beginning it. A letter that arrived recently from a friend of mine whose first novel got rave reviews opens with these words: "So painful coming into possession of a new novel. There is a deep agenda, and I sometimes think

I haven't the faintest clue what it is. Still, every day, here I am, at my table, facing it and struggling with lethargy." The material of a story offers itself to the writer like a house in which all the doors and windows are locked. Whose story is it? Whose voice does it belong to? The opening sentence is the key, the way into the house. It may let you in at the front door like a homeowner or at the window like a thief, but it lets you in.

For my angel story, I had no opening sentence. But I had a great many notes on angels, particularly those I deemed useful to writers. Uriel, the angel of poetry; and Raphael, the angel of healing, led the list. And how many angels there are, for every problem and purpose! There is an angel who presides over memory and an angel who presides over time, even an angel who presides over Monday. There is an angel for small birds and an angel for tame beasts, an angel for solitude and an angel for patience and an angel for hope. The angel who watches over footstools can offer you a pillar of light to support you, a gift that Hemingway and Virginia Woolf would have appreciated since both wrote standing up.

I also noted the angels who presided over conditions that writers pray to be spared. Michael, the angel of chaos and insomnia; Harbonah, the angel of annihilation; and Abaddon, the angel of the abyss.

But among the angels, who can really tell which are for us and which against us? There is an angel who presides over hidden things. Forgotten names, lost notes, misplaced drafts—does he hide them or find them? There is an angel of chance and an angel of odd events. Are they gifts or griefs, lucky accidents or lost opportunities?

Notice, I didn't say I wrote my story. I said, "worked on it." What did I really know about angels? How do we come to know things as writers? I looked at my notes, but no story came. What was I looking for? I made tea. I thought of how other writers prepared to face the blank page. Balzac drank fifty cups of coffee a day till it killed him; Disraeli put on evening clothes; George Cohan rented a Pullman-car drawing room and traveled till he was done with the book or story. Emerson took walks. Colette's husband locked her in her room, and Victor Hugo gave his clothes to his servant with instructions to return them when he was done.

After struggling with the story for three days, I understood the problem. This story had the shape of the one I'd just finished writing. What we've just written lays its shadow on the next work, and it can happen with any length, any genre. A friend who was working on her second novel told me, "It took me two years to break the spell of my first book when I started my second. I kept wanting to repeat what had worked so well. Combinations of characters, scenes." Writing is like panning for gold. You put your pan down close to the mother lode and scoop up a handful of gravel. You know the grains of ore would be sparkling in front of you if only you could see them. Knowing this, even when you find nothing but broken stones, it's hard to throw them away.

So I wrote a story about angels. I wrote badly. I was on the wrong track, but I didn't have the courage to throw those pages away, for then I'd have nothing. Keats was right. All writing is a form of prayer. Was anybody out there listening?

Let me say right now that I don't think anyone can command the angel to come, though I've known at least one person to try, a nun who told her first graders about the guardian angels they'd received at baptism and then said, "I want you all to move over and make room for your angels." Twenty-five first graders shifted to the right and made room for the incorporeal and the invisible. *That* is perfect faith. The nephew who told me the story takes a more skeptical view of angels now.

None of this would be worth telling if I hadn't promised my sister that I'd wash Mother's clothes at the laundromat, and what shouldn't happen did happen. I had a simple plan. I would sit with Mother till noon. While she ate her lunch in the dining room, I would carry the laundry basket over to the laundromat and read *The Art of Fiction* and work on my story while the clothes were spinning. And maybe I could take lunch down the street at Isaac's Vegetarian Deli. It had been closed all week, but a sign promised it would be open on Monday.

I arrived at Shady Park around eleven and headed for Mother's room. A thin, white-haired woman was walking toward me on crutches, leaning heavily on stout Miss Davidson, the physical therapist. Miss Davidson beckoned me over.

"I've been trying to get your mom to walk. She doesn't try. She won't even stand up for me. See if you can get her to make an effort."

"I'll do my best," I said.

"Now, Beulah here is doing fine," said Miss Davidson.

The woman on crutches nodded. "I walk every chance I get," she said. "Miss Davidson says, 'Well, how about heading back to your room now?' and I say, 'It hurts, but let's go just once more up and down the corridor.' I can't wait to go home."

Miss Davidson frowned at me. "Medicare won't pay for your mother's room if she's not taking part in the physical-therapy program."

"Is she doing any activities?" I asked hopefully.

"She likes the crafts," said Miss Davidson. "She made a purple flyswatter out of felt yesterday. And she had the kitten on her lap the whole day."

"What kitten?" I asked.

"Pet therapy," said Beulah. "Your mother wouldn't let anyone else have it. Kept it on her lap the whole time."

When I walked into her room, Mother was asleep in her chair.

"Ma," I said, "I hear you had a kitten."

She opened her eyes.

"What kitten?" she asked.

"She forgot already," said Beulah, leaning in the doorway. Mother turned to her.

"My husband taught for forty-seven years at the University of Michigan. We have a total of twenty-two degrees in our family—all from Michigan."

"Isn't that nice," said Beulah. "Now me, I never went to college. My papa worked in the steel mill, and so did my husband, till it shut down. I'm going downstairs in the wheelchair. They have Kool-Aid on the terrace."

We heard her thumping back to her room. Mother gave me an odd look. "Why are you carrying a box of soap?" she asked.

"I'm going to wash your clothes."

And I heaved the laundry basket onto one hip. Lavender plastic; my sister had picked it especially for her.

"You're a good girl," she said, and smiled. "Lord, I'm just an ordinary mother. How did I get two such wonderful daughters?"

I wheeled her downstairs, and we sat on the terrace with Beulah till lunchtime. The only other patient was a thin, silent man in a wheelchair; a young woman sat beside him, asking, "Grandpa, can you talk? Can you talk, Grandpa?"

"That's Mr. Levine," said Beulah. "He's a hundred and two. The president sent him a telegram." She leaned forward and whispered in my ear, "You ask him how old he is, and he shouts, 'A hundred and two!' There's not much else he knows. He has Alzheimer's. And he still has a full head of hair."

"What disease do I have?" asked Mother.

"You broke your hip," I said.

"I've had lots of broken bones," said Beulah. "Last year I broke my arm."

Mother stared down at her own arm, the scarred one, as if it had just been brought for her approval.

"How old it looks," she said softly.

The laundromat was nearly empty. A woman was sitting under the lone hair dryer reading a magazine from which the cover had been ripped away. I threw Mother's clothes in the machine, dialed it to Warm, and poured in the soap. I put *The Art of Fiction* and my box of Tide in the laundry basket and strolled half a block to Isaac's Vegetarian Deli.

The restaurant was tiny—no more than five tables. A sign on the wall read: Tel Aviv, Jerusalem, Ben Gurion Airport. Discover Your Roots!

Only one other customer, an elderly man in a black suit, was waiting at the takeout counter for his order. The two cooks wore yarmulkes, yet how different the same garment looked on each of them. The older man was clean shaven and middle-aged. When he chopped the onions, he seemed to be murdering them. He poured coffee as if it were poison. He shoved a plate of dumplings at the elderly man like a punishment. The younger cook had a thick blond beard and kindly blue eyes, and he loped from the stove to the icebox to the counter as if he had not a care in the world.

The menu over the counter listed vegetable soup and vegetarian pizza.

"I'll have soup," I said. "What kind of dumplings did you just give that man?"

"You won't like them," said the sour cook.

"I'll have them anyway," I said.

"Try one first," said the young cook, "and if you like it, I'll give you a plateful."

He handed me a dumpling on a paper plate. It tasted like nothing I'd ever eaten before or would want to eat again. I ordered a plate of them to spite the sour cook. The elderly gentleman took his paper plate, paused at a small rack on the wall, from which he plucked a greasy page. Out of curiosity, I took one also and found it was a page from the Jewish prayer book—Hebrew on one side, English on the other. There was also a pamphlet, *Thought for the Week,* so I took that as well and read it as I munched my dumplings: "A Thought for the Week: Love your fellow Jew as you love yourself."

Alas, I was not a Jew. They would feed me here, but they would not love me. I read on:

> Sidra Vayeishev. It is different at home (Part II). Last week we learned that our forefather Jacob did not feel "at home" in the world of material possessions. Knowing that he was only a temporary resident in this physical world he felt that his true "home" was in matters of the Neshama, in Torah and Mitzvos. The world with all its comforts, its palaces and mansions, is nothing more than a tent, erected during the journey of life to sleep over for a night, or rest for a day or two. And on a journey, after all, only the bare necessities of eating and sleeping are required; but when the journey is over and one comes home . . . Well, at home it's different.

When I'd finished the last greasy bite, I put the pamphlet and the prayer sheet in the rack and returned to the laundromat. The lights on the machine were off. The clothes were clean. So was the top of the machine.

The clothes basket, along with *The Art of Fiction* and my manuscript, had vanished.

Though the day was hot, I felt as cold as if I wore the wind for a cloak. A terrible calm washed over me, leaving me light-headed. Loss had numbed my capacity to rage.

Suddenly, among the *Reader's Digest*s on the folding table, I spied *The Art of Fiction*. I snatched it up. With shaking fingers I riffled through all the other magazines, shook them, and waited for my manuscript to come out of hiding like a mischievous child.

Nothing. On this occasion the angel who presides over hidden things was not on my side.

What else was there to do but walk across the street and sit on the bench at the bus stop and consider my life? When the elderly gentleman from Isaac's Deli sat next to me, I was scarcely aware of him till he began to edge closer.

"I notice the subject of your book," he said. "It is a subject dear to my heart. Are you a writer?"

"Yes," I said.

"Stories? You write stories?"

"Stories, a novel, poems," I said.

"I too wrote stories once," he said, "though I am not a writer now. I am a teacher. A teacher of American literature. But I have written stories."

My heart sank. He saw in me a kindred soul. Soon he would press his manuscript upon me. Yet he had used the past tense; perhaps he wrote stories no more. Had his inspiration run dry? Had he lost his memory?

"What kind of stories do you write," he asked, "if I may ask?"

"Short stories," I said.

"Forgive me," he said. "It's like asking the birds what kind of eggs they lay. Blue? Speckled? Large? Small?"

"Look," I said, "I can't really talk about my stories just now. Somebody just stole the only copy of the story I've been working on for weeks."

"You are sure somebody stole it?" he asked, as if such things did not happen in this world.

"I left it in the laundromat while I was eating lunch. And when I came back—"

"Excuse me," he interrupted, "but may I tell you a story? Long ago there lived in a north province in China a man good at interpreting events. This man had a son, and one day the son's best mare ran away and was taken by the nomads across the border. The son was distraught, but his father said, 'What makes you think this isn't a blessing?' Many months later, the horse returned, bringing with her a magnificent stallion. The son was delighted and mounted the horse but had scarcely set out for a ride when he fell and broke his hip. Again he was distraught, and again his father said, 'What makes you think this isn't a blessing?' Two years later the nomads invaded, and every able-bodied man marched to battle. All were lost. Only the lame son and the elderly father survived. What is blessing and what is disaster?"

"Somebody stole my story. That's a disaster," I said.

Two young women joined us on the bench till one murmured to the other, "I can't stand this heat. I'm going to the drugstore."

"What do you need in the drugstore?" asked the other.

"Nothing. It's air-conditioned," said the first. "We can look at magazines."

I was about to follow them when the elderly gentleman said: "Steinbeck's dog chewed the first half of his draft of *Of Mice and Men*. And Steinbeck forgave him, saying: 'I'm not sure Toby didn't know what he was doing when he ate that first draft. I have promoted Toby-dog to be lieutenant-colonel in charge of literature.' You know, I used to write stories. And I almost wrote a novel. I had three hundred pages written in a big notebook. And then the war came. During the war I lost everything."

"How terrible to lose a novel!" I cried. I meant to say, How terrible to lose everything.

He shook his head.

"Really, in my case, it was a blessing. I wanted to write a family history, a *bildungsroman*. Thomas Mann was my hero. I had notes, a family tree, plans, hundreds of plans. But in my heart of hearts I knew my novel sounded wooden. A wise man said, 'A writer with a fixed idea is like a goose trying to hatch a stone.' In nineteen-forty, I was sent to Ravensbrück. All my life my teachers told me not to daydream. Now it was my salvation. Can you outline a dream? Would it be worth dreaming if you could? In that terrible place I let my mind wander, and my characters came back to me, not as I saw them in my notes and plans, but as they saw themselves, full of memories and longings. I understood their real story at last. I turned no one away. Does the sea refuse a single river? Have you heard of Van Der Post and his explorations of Africa?"

"No," I said. "Sorry."

"Never mind. He tells of the time he traveled to a village where a great hunter lived. When he arrived, he found the hunter sitting motionless. And the villagers said, 'Don't interrupt him. He is doing work of the utmost importance. He is making clouds.' "

"Did you finish your novel?" I asked. I have a weakness for happy endings.

"How could I finish it? We had no paper. No pens. But we had tongues. So I became a storyteller instead of a writer. I no longer thought of plots, only of voice. Of whose story I was telling. When I hear the voice, I know the story will find me. Storytellers do not lose their stories, except when they die. I like to start my stories in the old style: *Once upon a time*. *Once upon a time* is a promise, a promise of a story, and I try to keep my promises. Of course, not everyone agrees with me about these methods. My son, for example. He's a TV writer. Weekends, he wants to write the great American novel, but he doesn't know how to get started. One day he calls me from New York, all excited. 'I've just signed a contract to write the bible!' Naturally I'm interested. He goes on to say that this bible is not from God, of course. This is the book TV scriptwriters use when they're doing a new series of shows. It describes characters, it describes place, it describes adventures.

" 'And for what show are you writing a bible?' I ask my son.

" 'It's a miniseries,' he says. 'It's called *The Further Adventures of Alice in Wonderland*.'

" 'How can that be?' I say. 'There is only one Lewis Carroll.'

" 'Yes, Papa, but there are five scriptwriters. They'll make up the other adventures. But they can write only about what they know. I'm going to write them a detailed description of Wonderland and the characters.' What do you think, fellow scribbler? Is it a good idea, *The Further Adventures of Alice in Wonderland*?"

"I don't know," I said. "What happened to your son?"

"My son read the Alice books carefully. He mapped the terrain, noted the architecture, the dangers, the geography, the birds and animals. He wrote out character studies of everyone mentioned in the books. And he got paid well. And suddenly a brilliant idea struck him. Why not write a bible for his great unwritten American novel? How much easier it would be to start his novel if he had a detailed knowledge of his characters. Hadn't his English teachers always said, 'Write about what you know'?"

"My teachers said the same thing," I said with a laugh.

"They all say it," said the elderly gentleman. "I even said it to my students. But I didn't mean my students should write such a bible. If you take everyone's advice, you'll build a crazy house. My son wrote out descriptions of all his characters and their locale. Then he wrote the first two chapters and showed them to me. 'Aaron,' I said, 'how can I tell you? This is from your head, not your heart. It's predictable. No surprises. Even God is surprised by the actions of his creatures.'

" 'I've put a lot of time into this,' he said.

" 'The nest is done, but the bird is dead,' I told him. 'You should take a lesson from your Lewis Carroll. He was a storyteller. I know for a fact that when he sent his Alice down the rabbit hole, he didn't know what would happen next. That white rabbit was a gift from Providence. We should follow Providence, not force it.' He's intelligent, my Aaron, but he thinks too much. He needs intelligence to keep him from hindering himself so that he is free to do amazing things. I tell him to watch Charlie Chaplin. You have seen his great film *Modern Times?*"

"A long time ago," I said, hoping he wouldn't quiz me on it.

"Maybe you remember, near the end, Charlie has to go on the stage and sing a song. And now he can't remember the words. So Paulette Goddard writes the words on his cuff. He goes onstage, he tries to read them, he's hopeless. Not a sound out of him. He's paralyzed. And then Paulette Goddard calls out, 'Never mind the words. Just sing.' "

"I think that kind of thing happens only when you tell stories," I said, "not when you write them."

"It can also happen when you write them," he said. "You have two choices. You can arrange the material, with outlines. Or you can arrange yourself. I see you looking at the laundromat. You have business there?"

"I forgot to put my mom's clothes in the dryer."

"And you want to see if the thief returned your manuscript," he added.

"Yes," I agreed.

Suddenly I remembered my promise.

"Excuse me," I said, rising. "Do you know a good shoe store?"

"From writing to shoes!" he said, and laughed.

"I have to run. I promised my mother I'd buy some new shoes."

"Are you in such a hurry?" he exclaimed. "Let me tell you about a man who set out to buy himself shoes. He measured his foot and put the measurements away. When he got to the market, he found he'd left the measurements at home. He chose a pair of shoes and hurried home for the measurements, but when he returned, the market was closed. He never got the shoes, of course. And that night he dreamed his feet asked him, 'Why didn't you trust us? Why did you trust the measurements more than your own feet?' "

We stood up in unison.

"There's a department store one street over," he said. "But all shoe stores are good if you need shoes."

I didn't go shopping for shoes, and I didn't find my manuscript. When I arrived at Shady Park, Mother was not in her room. She had been wheeled into the TV room. She was asleep, her head nearly on her chest; she had been left at a long empty table with her back to the TV. Probably she had told the attendant that she didn't like television. The other chairs were all facing the set as if their occupants were worshipping it.

I rushed in and turned her chair around. "Wake up, Ma. We're going back to your room."

But Mr. Levine's chair was stuck in the doorway, blocking it. He was making helpless swoops with his hands, trying to move the wheels.

"Let me help you," I said, and pushed him through.

Instantly a ripple of movement started behind me as if I had waked the very walls.

"Lady, can you help me?"

"Miss, can you get me out of here? Miss!"

Heads lifted, hands waved.

"Miss!"

I can't help them all, I thought.

"Mother, do you want to look at the box of photographs with me?"

"I want to lie down," she said.

What angel was present in the room with us on that evening? The angel of chance or the angel of memory? The angel of time or the angel of hidden things? After I'd put away her dresses, clean but crumpled from being carried in my arms, I sat on the edge of her bed and flipped through the box of snapshots. Tucked in among the pictures were Christmas cards. Mother never threw away a Christmas card that had a photograph on it. I held up a picture of an elderly couple standing in front of the Taj Mahal.

"Who in thunder are they?" exclaimed Mother.

"I don't know," I said. "Let me read you the writing on the back. 'We visited fourteen countries and had a wonderful time. Love, Dorothy and Jack.' "

"Are both my parents dead?" asked Mother.

"Oh, Ma, you know they died a long time ago. If they were alive, they'd be a hundred and twenty."

I pulled out another picture and held it up. It showed a middle-aged woman standing on what appeared to be a cistern and smiling. I turned the photograph over and read the scrawled inscription: " 'This is your old Aunt Ruth standing by the well. Clark covered it over for me and put in running water, hot and cold. He also made the driveway you can see behind me, to the left.' "

Mother's face brightened.

"I remember that well," she said. "There was a pump on Grandpa's farm in Iowa. Oh, he had acres and acres of the best farmland in the county. And when the men were working in the fields, Grandma would fill a bucket of water from that pump. And she'd send me out with the bucket and dipper to give the men a drink. And it seemed like such a long walk coming and going. I was dying of thirst by the time I got back to the house. And Grandma wouldn't let me pour myself a drink from the pump right off. No. She made me hold my wrists under the spout, and she'd pump and pump the water over them. To cool my blood, she said, so that the cold drink wouldn't give me a stomachache. Lord, how good that cold water felt. And how good it tasted."

I'd never heard her tell this story. How many other stories lay hidden in her heart, waiting for a listener to wake them?

Suddenly I understood my real task. I would lay my angel story aside and forget about it for a while. Tomorrow I would bring a notebook and start writing down her memories. I would have to be patient. Memory has nothing to do with outlines and everything to do with accidents.

On my way home I stopped once more at the laundromat and couldn't believe my eyes. There on top of the fateful washing machine stood the clothes basket. And safe in its plastic lavender embrace nestled my story.

I pulled it out and turned the pages, checking them for bruises. I counted the pages. I pulled up a chair and reread them.

Was the angel of hope responsible for what happened next?

I threw the entire manuscript in the wastebasket. I would take Rilke's advice: "If the angel deigns to come, it will be because you have convinced him, not by tears, but by your horrible resolve to be a beginner."

Voices. Voices. That night, before I fell asleep, I heard the voices of my characters, though faintly, like a conversation accidentally picked up on a long-distance line. I did not let them know I was listening.

The next morning I set out for Shady Park Manor with a light heart and was pleasantly surprised to meet my storyteller coming out of the synagogue at the end of the block.

"You are going to visit your mother? May I walk with you as far as Jerry's Good and Used?"

"What's Jerry's Good and Used?"

"Jerry has this and that of everything. His specialty is baseball cards. He calls last night and says, 'I have a treasure. Something you want very much, a card of the great Japanese ball player Sadaharu Oh.' He asks me why I want a card of Sadaharu Oh. I tell him that I want a picture of the man who wrote in his autobiography not about winning but about waiting. Waiting, he says in that book, is the most active state of all. It is the beginning of all action. Did you find your manuscript?"

"I found it. And I threw it away. I'm starting over. This time I'll wait for the story to find me. Like you said yesterday."

I expected my new acquaintance to offer his congratulations, but he did not.

"The freedom of the dream doesn't mean doing nothing. You still have to sit down every day and write. What if the angel came and you were out shopping for shoes? God helps the drowning sailor, but he must row. You have a long journey ahead of you. And it starts with one footstep."

"It feels more like an ending than a beginning," I said.

"Endings and beginnings—are they so far from each other? When I was in Ravensbrück, I was chosen to die. Only because someone among the killers recognized me was I saved. Now when I tell my stories, I remember that moment. It makes the telling more urgent. How is your mother?"

"Fine, I guess. Just very tired."

"You know, when I was little, my mother would put me to sleep by describing rooms in all the houses she'd lived in. And so many things happened in those rooms. Now you can hardly find a house in which someone has died or been born. It all happens away from us, in big hospitals."

"My mother told me a story yesterday," I said. And I described to him my mother's journey to the harvest fields with the bucket of water and the journey back to the well and the cold water on her wrists.

He was silent for so long that I felt I had said something foolish.

"The cold water—it's such an unimportant detail," I remarked.

"Unimportant?" he exclaimed. "That is why it's worth remembering. When I was young, I fell in love with a girl named Hilda who happened to be a twin. I asked her to go out with me. She agreed to go but only if I could tell her apart from her sister. I studied her face for several minutes. Then she ran and got her twin. Hilda had a blue vein on the bridge of her nose. Unimportant, a blue vein, but when I spied it, I knew I was saved."

"I'll save that detail about the cold water for my next story," I assured him.

He wagged a finger at me. "Don't save it. Use it, use it now. You just threw out your life savings. This is no time for prudence."

We passed Jerry's Good and Used. My storyteller did not go in. Instead he kept pace with me up the hill to Shady Park Manor.

"May I tell you a story as we take this little walk together? Long ago, when wizards still walked the length and breadth of the earth, there arrived in the world of the dead a great magician.

" 'Why have you come here?' asked the Mistress of the Dead.

"The magician explained that when he was building his boat, he found he could not finish it without four magic words and that he had not been able to find them, however far he traveled.

" 'The Lord of the Dead will never teach you his spells,' answered the Mistress of the Dead.

"But the magician could not give up the task of finishing his boat. He wandered here and there until one day he met a shepherd who told him to seek out the giant.

" 'In his vast mouth there are a hundred magic words. You will have to go down into his enormous belly, and there you will learn marvels. But it's not easy to get there. You must go along a path leaping on the points of women's needles and over a crossroad paved with sharp swords and down a third road made of the blades of heroes' axes.'

"But the magician was determined to try it. He would do anything to find those four words and finish his boat. Four words! Marvelous words! Would you believe I once bought a photography book because of a single sentence? I was standing in Tucker's—it's a block down the street from us—and I opened up a book and read the epigraph on the first page. It was the beginning and the ending of *Finnegans Wake:*

> A way a lone a last a loved
> along the riverrun,
> past Eve and Adam's[2]

Right away I wanted to read *Finnegans Wake*. But Tucker's didn't have it. And the library was closed for a week. But how could I live without those words? So I bought the photography book. I bought it for those words."

We arrived at Shady Park.

"It is good you are listening to your mother."

"I'm going to write her memories down. I don't want to forget them."

"If you forget a few, don't worry. What you need will come back to you. We don't really understand something until we have forgotten it. Live in your roots, not in your branches."

I took the elevator to the second floor. When I stepped out, a nurse hurried up to me.

"Your mother had a seizure last night. We phoned for the ambulance just an hour ago. Call Dr. Rubin right away. You can use the phone at the nurses' station."

The voice of medical authority at the other end of the phone named the problem: status epilepticus. Dr. Rubin explained he had given her Valium and phenobarbital.

"It took us over an hour to stop her seizure. Now she's asleep."

"Did she have a stroke?"

"This morning I thought yes. When I looked at the CAT scan, I thought no. Her brain is shrunken, and there's an abnormal pattern of electric ions. It's probably caused by the little strokes she's had earlier."

"I'll be right over."

I hung up, and the nurse touched my arm.

"I'm so sorry," she said. "Let me call you a cab."

I waited downstairs for the cab. The receptionist was changing the bulletin board, posting the new activities: Bingo, sensory stimulation, current events, patio outing.

A way a lone a last a loved along the riverrun.

Dr. Rubin and I are standing by my mother's bed in the intensive-care section. Mother is sleeping under the watchful gaze of the IV and the blood-pressure basket hanging over her bed, its black tubes coiled into a nest. Over the basket a large plastic bottle bubbles and quakes. This is not the first time I have seen Mother in intensive care.

"When do you think she'll wake up?" I ask.

The doctor shrugs.

"Who knows? It could be tomorrow. It could be in ten minutes. Or it could be never."

I reach out and touch her hair, still soft and wavy, and the translucent skin on her temple: pale freckled silk. The doctor pulls away the plastic respirator that covers the center of her face with a clear green beak, and her sunken cheeks flutter in and out like the throat of a frightened bird. A tube snakes out of her nose, ready for her next feeding. Her mouth is a small black hole. The doctor leans close to her face, as if he might kiss her. Then he pries open her eyelids and looks deeply into her pupils and calls her by name.

Two green-gray coins stare back at him as cold and indifferent as the eyes of a fish. I feel my knees growing weak, and I sit down fast on the edge of her bed.

"Can she hear us now?"

"Possibly. There's no way of knowing for sure."

When he leaves us alone together, I take her hand, frail as the claw of a wren. The IV has left a deep bruise on her arm. How old it looks, this arm, limp when I lift it, a mottled mineral brown across which white scars move like the shapes of ancient beasts.

I know I will never see her alive again. I do not know if she can hear. I put my mouth close to her ear and tell her I love her. I thank her for telling me about the cold water. I tell her that I lost my story in Pittsburgh, a story about angels. I lost it at the laundromat, and I met a man who told me how to find it again. Maybe he wasn't a man at all, maybe he was the story angel? He did not have wings, but who needs wings in Pittsburgh? Though my mouth is touching her ear, I feel my mother going further and further away. I want to talk to her till she is out of earshot. Though she is traveling with empty hands, I do not want my mother, who has given me so much, to leave with an empty heart. I give her an angel, a daughter, and herself. And I give her my promise to save them: *once upon a time.*

NOTES

[1] John Gardner, *The Art of Fiction* (New York: Knopf, 1984), 31.

[2] James Joyce, *Finnegans Wake* (New York: Viking/Penguin Centennial Edition, 1982).

SOMETHING THAT

WILL LAST

●　　●　　●　　●　　●　　●　　●　　●　　●

Let me start by telling you what you won't read in this chapter. You won't read about dreams and how writers use them in stories. You won't learn how in my novel *Things Invisible to See* I included dreams told to me by my Aunt Bon. When her daughter Sue recognized those dreams in my book, she was surprised and pleased.

"That dream of my mother's, the one in which she goes to heaven and back," said Sue, "it's nice. But did you ever hear about the time she woke up and saw twelve angels standing around her bed with candles in their hands? Come over for a visit, and I'll tell you that story."

The night of my mother's funeral, I heard bits and pieces of that story. Sue and her husband, Ben, had driven from Grosse Pointe to my mother's house in Ann Arbor. The house was full of cousins and second cousins, in-laws and grandchildren, who had flown in from Washington, New York, Montana, Texas, Pennsylvania. English is peculiarly deficient in words for family relationships. Ben, for example. Was he my cousin? My cousin-in-law? Did it matter? He was family. I let it go at that.

In the morning we committed my mother's body to the earth, and in the evening we returned to my mother's house and reminded ourselves that she was happiest when the family was gathered in this place enjoying one another's company. It was June, the beginning of hot weather in Ann Arbor, and all the windows and doors stood open. We sat around the coffee table in the living room and played Ubi Sunt? ("Where Are——"), a board game involving maps and a knowledge of geography. Where is the capital of Brazil? Where is the capital of Nigeria? The last time I saw Ben he was shouting *"Ubi sunt!"* and pointing to Paris on a map that looked much too colorful to be taken seriously. I had forgotten the capital cities of all except a handful of countries, but I hadn't forgotten the François Villon poem "The Ballad of Dead Ladies," with its famous refrain:

> Where is Echo, beheld of no man,
> Only heard on river and mere,
> She whose beauty was more than human? . . .
> But where are the snows of yester-year?[1]

If Villon were alive today, he might use a different metaphor to show our mortality: Where are the voices telling good news and bad to the message machines so many of us have added to our telephones? *Ubi sunt?*

Erased.

I have been suspicious of these devices ever since my husband, Eric, and I stayed in the apartment of a friend whose answering machine, he assured us, required no special attention. For days the machine was silent, sullen, and suspiciously well behaved. On our last night in the apartment, it woke us at two in the morning in response to a call and shouted all the messages it had been storing up for a week, filling the dark with a cacophony of voices: a schizophrenic confessing to two groggy and astonished listeners.

Nevertheless, after years of railing against such devices, Eric and I broke down and bought one. We set it up, turned it on, and forgot about it—until early the next morning, when it woke us with the voice of my niece calling from Ann Arbor.

"Hello. This is Margaret. Sue called to say that Ben was killed by a sniper last night on his way home from a business meeting."

I sprang out of bed, lunged for the phone, missed it, and called her back. Sue had asked Margaret to call other members of the family and tell them about Ben's death.

"His picture was on Channel Two news," said Margaret. "I videotaped it."

Many calls later I was able to piece the story together. Ben was driving home from a meeting at the Bayview Yacht Club. The car was new, a Cadillac. Did Ben especially admire Cadillacs? Probably not. There is an understanding among those who work in the auto-manufacturing business: If you have the account, you drive the car. Ben had the Cadillac account and drove, therefore, a midnight blue Cadillac with red upholstery and a telephone. He took the river road, through Bayview. He might have chosen a safer route, but the river road was the fastest, and he was eager to be home. I imagine he sped up as he entered the deserted block with its empty Chrysler plant and its lonely stretch of asphalt. Not far ahead stretched the green lawns of Grosse Pointe and the mansions looking out on the trim yachts bobbing over the white-capped water. Saint Paul's also faced the water; Ben and Sue went to early Mass there on Sundays.

When Ben spied a tree limb blocking the middle of the street, he did not climb out of the car to drag it aside. Ben was born and raised in Detroit, and he knew about the homemade roadblocks car thieves set for the unwary. Climb out of your car to move that roadblock, and chances are you'll never see that car again. Ben sped up and tried to swerve around it. Did he see the man jump out of the dark and fire, point-blank, the bullet that ripped the door of the car, passed through one lung, and entered his heart? Ben's last act on earth was to pick up the telephone and call his son.

These were the bare facts. But for anyone with imagination—and we all have imagination in these circumstances—it's ourselves we see in that car, and the bare facts are only the beginning. The facts of Ben's death haunted me all day, as if my own fate were stalking me, just out of sight. Our ancestors spoke of fate as three goddesses. The first chooses your life, the second spins the thread, the third cuts it. When I think of fate, I don't see three goddesses. I see a writer who dreams up my story, writes it, and one day will finish it.

Life as story. Crazy? Perhaps. But what are our lives if not stories? The realist who first told the Grimm's fairy tale "Godfather Death" ended the story with the character's life as story—the better to wring our hearts:

> . . . Death . . . walked up to the physician with long strides and said: "All is over with you, and now the lot falls on you," and seized him so firmly with his ice-cold hand, that he could not resist, and led him into a cave below the

earth. There he saw how thousands and thousands of candles were burning in countless rows, some large, some medium-sized, others small. . . . "See," said Death, "these are the lights of men's lives. The large ones belong to children, the medium-sized ones to married people in their prime, the little ones belong to old people; but children and young folks likewise have often only a tiny candle." "Show me the light of my life," said the physician, and he thought it would still be very tall. Death pointed to a little end which was just threatening to go out, and said: "Behold, it is there." "Ah, dear godfather," said the horrified physician, "Light a new one for me. . . ." Death behaved as if he were going to fulfill his wish, and took hold of a tall new candle; but . . . purposely made a mistake in fixing it, and the little piece fell down and was extinguished. Immediately the physician fell on the ground, and now he himself was in the hands of Death.[2]

It is surely no accident that some of our finest writers have been doctors or students of medicine: Chekhov, Rabelais, and Keats, Somerset Maugham and William Carlos Williams, Walker Percy and Robert Coles. What Dr. John Stone, a poet and teacher at the Emory School of Medicine, has to say about literature and the training of doctors is good medicine for any writer:

Literature, indeed, can have a kind of laboratory function. In other words, the medical ear must be properly trained to hear stories—a medical history, after all, is a short story. In this sense, a person's life can be thought of as a series of stories, coalescing over time to form the most idiosyncratic novel ever written. The good doctor must learn to listen for the real message in these stories of his patients, to read them, as Robert Frost used to say, "with a listening ear."[3]

Writers too are listeners, both to the stories people tell them and to the stories they tell themselves. As writers, what are we listening for that helps us shape our material? Let me go back to the story of Ben's death.

Neither the television nor my niece could give me enough facts to put the whole story together. Eric suggested I call Sue herself. Is there any among us who is not tongue-tied when confronted with someone who has suffered a terrible loss? Grief has no special syntax or vocabulary. To bend ordinary language to your own subtle purposes—it's like trying to mend a wedding dress with an ice pick.

Nevertheless, I called my cousin, and she came to the phone.

"It's on the front page," she said. " 'Wealthy Grosse Pointe Executive Killed.' 'Wealthy'—ha! People keep coming by with food. You can't imagine how much food we have in this house."

In a calm voice she informed me that Ben's wake would be on Saturday—"No viewing, just people dropping by"—the Rosary on Sunday, the funeral Mass on Monday, and the burial on Tuesday.

"Ben went out the front door and he never came back," she said. "Channel Two has set up cameras in our front yard. We had to pull the drapes. I never liked those drapes when we moved into this house. But I'm awfully glad for them now."

And she burst into tears.

Earlier I mentioned the bare facts of the story. But, of course, to a writer no facts are bare. In the depths of sorrow and the heights of danger, we may find ourselves both weeping and watching ourselves weep. The English novelist Arnold Bennett once boasted that the death scene of one of his characters could not be improved upon "because I took infinite pains over it. All the time my father was dying, I was at the bedside making copious notes."[4] Of course, we find this appalling. But who among us does not take copious notes in his head even as he gives himself over to grief and fear?

Let me tell you a story. When I was a student at Stanford, I too met violence at the hands of a stranger. I was biking home from the library at night through the palm grove that surrounds the campus when a man leapt out from the trees and knocked me to the ground. His intention, I discovered later in court, was to kill me first and rape me later. He put his hands around my neck, tightened them, and waited for me to die. Neither of us knew that over our struggle the light on my bicycle was shining into the tops of the palm trees like a wayward star.

At this point the story sounds like the script for a bad television series. The captain and the quarterback of the Stanford football team were returning from a movie and spied a mysterious beam cutting through the foliage over their heads. So it came to pass that I found myself in the police station with the two football players who had saved me and the policeman who was writing up the report.

The policeman asked, "Were you raped?"

"No," I said.

"Step into the other room and make sure," he said.

I stared at him in bewilderment. "But why? There's absolutely no question about this."

The policeman sighed and put down his pen. "It's part of the procedure. There has to be an inspection," he said. "I can't leave it blank on the form."

There was no dissuading him, so I stepped into the back room of the police barracks. Suddenly the writer part of me took over. I'd never been in a police barracks, and who knew when I might want to write a story requiring just such a scene? I glanced at the desk, the notices on the wall, the calendar, the bookshelves. Instead of books they held bowling trophies, a flock of small golden men perched on marble blocks leaning forward in unison, hands extended, each hand sending a golden ball down an invisible alley.

These are the bare facts. But bare facts are not stories. Stories are facts as they happen to people, and I could not write the story of what happened to me in the palm grove until I'd found the voice to tell it, the voice of someone who was like me and yet not like me at all. We speak of finding the right voice for a story or novel. The characters, the scenes, the events gather in our heads like the cast of a play on opening night. But the voice is the director, without whom the performers may wait for years on the dark stage before the curtain rises. I do not think we find these voices. I think they find us— sometimes only after we have lived with the characters for years and even abandoned them.

It took ten years for the voice that could tell that story to find me. And what the voice gave me was not a short story but a poem, "Clearing the Air":

> It's been ten years since you tried to kill me.
> Biking home one night, I saw only your legs
> stepping behind a tree, then you fell on my throat
> like a cat. My books crashed the birds out of sleep.
> We rolled in the leaves like lovers. My eyes popped
> like Christmas lights, veins snapped, your teeth wore
> my blood, your fingers left bars on my neck.

I can't remember your name,
and I saw your face only in court.
You sat in a box, docile as old shoes.
And I, who had never felt any man's weight,
sometimes felt yours for nights afterwards.

Well, I'm ready to forgive
and I don't want to forget.
Sometimes I tell myself we met
differently, on a train. You give me
a Batman comic and show me your passport.
I have nothing but my report card,

but I offer my mother's fudge for the grapes
rotting the one paper bag you carry.
In my tale you are younger and loved.
Outside you live in a thousand faces
and so do your judges, napping in parks,
rushing to fires, folded like bats on the truck,

mad and nude in a white Rolls
pinching dollars and leather behinds.
Burned from a tree by your betters, you take
to the streets and hang in the dark like a star,
making me see your side, waking me
with the blows and the weight of it.[5]

To understand all is to forgive, said Flaubert. He might have added
that such understanding takes time. Only to a few people does it come
naturally, and I am not one of them. To William Carlos Williams it

came naturally—if we are to believe Ezra Pound. "Where I see scoundrels and vandals," writes Pound, "he sees a spectacle or an ineluctable process of nature."[6]

What did I see when I heard the news of Ben's death? Scoundrels and vandals. Certainly nothing so objective as a process of nature.

When I arrived at my cousin's house, the living room was so full of friends laughing and chatting that I felt as if I were at a New Year's Eve party. All afternoon the flowers kept coming; baskets ascended the steps leading to the second floor like a procession of debutantes waiting to be photographed. A large colored photograph of Ben stood on the piano. Safe in his gold frame, Ben seemed to be watching us, making sure the glasses were filled and the guests were happy. On shelves and coffee tables, the model trains he loved seemed to have stopped in their tracks. In the kitchen, a headline caught my eye: "Slain Driver an Avid Sailor, Taught Sport to Young." Someone had left the clipping from the *Detroit Free Press* on the counter:

> Half a block from the blue waters of Lake St. Clair where he loved to sail and taught many others, family and friends gathered in shock Friday at the home of Benjamin Gravel, who was killed in an apparently random shooting on a Detroit street.
>
> Gravel was returning to his home in Grosse Pointe Farms from a meeting at the Bayview Yacht Club around 10 P.M. Thursday when he was shot in the chest as he drove north through a construction zone on Conner, just south of Jefferson.
>
> Police said the shot was fired from outside the car, on Gravel's left side.

Gravel died about an hour later at Saint John's Hospital in Detroit.

At the end of the article, a single sentence jumped out at me: "Gravel was asked to serve as a judge in the America's Cup race in 1987 but had to decline the offer because he could not leave his job as a manufacturer's representative in the auto industry."

Ben a judge in the America's Cup race? I hadn't known that. Reading the article and the obituary, I felt as if I were meeting Ben for the first time. And I thought of a much earlier meeting with Ben, not my first but nearly so, the summer I graduated from college. My graduation present from my parents was a trip to Europe. Ben was in the army, stationed in Germany, and he and Sue were not yet married. Sue asked me to look him up.

We met in a beer hall in Heidelberg. Most of the other customers were older men. Ben and I sat down at a long table opposite one of them, who introduced himself as a veteran of the Second World War. Hundreds of questions flooded my mind, and I didn't dare ask any of them: What did you know? What did you do and to whom did you do it? I could not rid myself of the thought that if Ben had been born a few generations earlier, the man sitting before me might have killed him at Dunkerque or Ardennes. But now the young soldier and the old one were smiling at each other like the best of friends. I scanned Ben's face. Where I saw a scoundrel, he saw a human being, part of the ineluctable process of nature that has nothing to do with history or politics. At that moment I learned something about traveling light and how little baggage we really need to get where we're going.

Tourists learn this more easily than writers.

The writer as outside observer and the writer as inside participant are like two sisters destined to fight with each other from the moment they are born. Let us imagine Miss Experience and Miss Gatherer have just entered the door of my cousin's house, a place they have often visited on more cheerful occasions. Miss Experience says, "What a lovely room! You've redecorated it!" Miss Gatherer says, "How much did you pay for this sofa? Where did you get it? Is your dress real silk?"

My cousin announces that Father Murphy has arrived to say the Rosary, and everyone sits down. Father Murphy begins by praising Ben the sailor and Ben the family man, proud of his son, whose photograph he carried in his wallet. The guests who have brought rosaries take them out of pockets and purses. Miss Experience has chosen a seat on a sofa near the back of the room. When Father Murphy begins to pray, she folds her hands. All around her tumble the words, one after another, like wings brushing her ears.

Miss Gatherer has found a seat in front, close to the priest; she doesn't want to miss a thing. Since she is a Protestant, she must work harder to remember the words as she listens for the images and metaphors that will help her shape the story she wants to tell. Indeed, she is already composing the story, editing, selecting what is useful to her. She cannot take notes—even she has some sense of propriety— but she makes a mental note of everything in the room: family pictures on the piano, model trains on the coffee table, baskets of flowers on the stairs. To fix the priest's eulogy in her mind, she memorizes key words that will recall the main points: *boat, wallet.*

Later, when the sisters compare their impressions, Miss Gatherer is dismayed to discover that she can remember the key words but not what they point to. She can list nearly everything in the living room, but she knows she could have done this at any other time. Since her list does not include feelings, it tells her nothing of what made this day different from all other days. She feels as if someone had reached into a long-hidden tomb and handed her an exquisite tapestry that crumbled to dust when she held it to the light. Time, which preserved it, also destroyed it.

And what does Miss Experience recall of the afternoon? Why, everything. She is astonished that her sister remembers so little. She too noted the room and its contents, for it takes a long time to say the rosary, and even those for whom piety is a calling do not attend to every word. What was she doing during her lapses? She was day-dreaming, woolgathering. Her gaze rested on the bowl of pink tulips on the coffee table, and her mind roamed back to the last time she saw that table, at Christmas. On it Sue had arranged the Nativity scene Ben had sent her from Germany. The stable, the star, the angels, the Wise Men, the shepherds, Mary, the Baby—all the principals were present except Joseph. Miss Experience remembered asking what had happened to Joseph.

"I lent him to our next-door neighbor when she was trying to sell her house," Sue replied. "If you bury a statue of Saint Joseph on the property, a house will sell right away. The market is awful around here, but she sold her house in a week."

The downside of this arrangement, she added, was that Joseph's mortal part, being papier-mâché, had rotted away, leaving nothing behind but his head. Well-meaning friends had brought her replace-ments, and she soon had half a dozen Josephs: plaster, wood, and plastic—a polygamy of husbands for Mary.

"But I gave them all away," she said. "None of them belonged to Mary like the one she'd lost."

Hail Mary: Miss Experience's mind returns to the present moment and to Father Murphy. Back and forth between past and present she moves, like a seamstress stitching, reinforcing, reworking the tapestry of these events, binding them to one another by many different threads.

Her subject is not the funeral but the human condition. Miss Gatherer's approach is rather like that of an inexperienced doctor or a first-year resident who lets himself become bogged down in circumstantial details. What Dr. Robert Coles says he learned from one of his teachers in medical school applies to writers as well as doctors:

> I slowly began to realize that we doctors had become diggers, trying hard to follow treasure maps in hopes of discovering gold. . . . If we didn't know, we knew what it was that we wanted to know and *would* know, once we'd made our discovery. . . .
>
> Dr. Ludwig urged us to let the story itself be our discovery. . . . He urged me to be a good listener in the special way a story requires: note the manner of presentation; the development of plot, character; the addition of new dramatic sequences; the emphasis accorded to one figure or another. . . . Their story, yours, mine—it's what we all carry with us on this trip we take, and we owe it to each other to respect our stories and learn from them.[7]

The difference between Miss Gatherer and Miss Experience is the difference between a handful of details and a real story. The details alone are like shells picked up at the beach. What looks so luminous in the water turns parched and chalky on the land. Details for a writer are parched when we isolate them from our feelings. They are luminous when we preserve them in the medium of memory. Nobody describes the difficulty of keeping our past intact better than Proust: "It is a labour in vain to attempt to recapture it: all the efforts of our intellect must prove futile. The past is hidden somewhere . . . beyond the reach of intellect. . . . Will it ultimately reach the clear surface of my consciousness, this memory, this old, dead moment . . . out of the very depths of my being?"[8]

What has happened here? The process of gathering has shifted from the surface to the depths, the well from which all stories come. And though we are not concerned with the healing power of stories, I think what doctors and therapists have said about the way stories heal children also describes the way stories happen to writers. Through nondirected play, says storyteller-therapist Elizabeth Radecki, children find their stories: "From week to week, if you just let the stories come out, you can listen to them and see an unfolding."[9]

Whole, resonant—isn't that what all writers want their stories to be? Don't we all want to rise from our desks with the feeling that we have written not out of what we know but out of more than we know? Isn't one of the objections to minimalism in fiction simply this: that the writer has gathered from the surface and not from the depths?

Let me tell you a story.

The first funeral I ever attended was that of my grandmother, who died when I was a sophomore in college. I'd never seen a dead person before except in the movies. At the funeral parlor, I peered into the coffin and tried to connect the body lying in front of me with the woman who had lived with us, on and off, and given us both joy and suffering. Quite unconsciously my hand snaked out and touched my grandmother's face.

When I stepped back from the coffin, I nearly bumped into my father. My father was a man of great feeling. He was also a scientist whose vocation had trained him to gather facts.

"What did it feel like?" he asked.

He was not asking, What did you feel like in the presence of this woman, but, What did her flesh feel like? He knew I alone, of all the people in the room, could both understand the question and answer it, because writers and scientists share the curse of detachment in the midst of emotion. And writers must know the look and feel of the visible world of the flesh if they are to describe the invisible world of the spirit.

Several months ago I was browsing in a bookshop and a curious title caught my eye: *How to Capture Live Authors and Bring Them to Your Schools*. The owner of the bookshop assured me it was a good book, and though I did not read it I have no reason to doubt her. The purpose of bringing authors and their readers together, she told me, is to encourage students to write. I hope very much there will be a sequel called *How to Capture Dead Authors,* since there are many writers I would hate to see excluded from schools because the fine print at the bottom of the lease on life we are born with says it is not renewable.

Of that group, whom would I hope to capture? I'd go after the anonymous tellers of folktales, because I know of no other literature that can teach writers so much about shaping narrative. Let me tell you how I invited a particular story to visit me and what Ben's death taught me about making that story my own. The story is "Beauty and the Beast." It's the well-loved story of a rich merchant with three daughters, the youngest of whom is called Beauty. The story begins when his ships are lost at sea, and the family, suddenly impoverished, is forced to move into the country. When word reaches the merchant that one of his ships has been found, he returns to the city, but not before asking his daughters what presents he should bring for them. The oldest two beg for gold and jewels. Beauty, not wishing to burden her father with an expensive request, asks for a rose. On his way home, a storm drives him into the woods, which is no doubt as lovely and dangerous as the palm grove mentioned earlier in which I escaped danger of a different kind. To the merchant's relief, the mysterious mansion where he takes shelter appears to be empty. A good dinner, a new suit of clothes, a soft bed—every comfort is offered him by invisible servants. But the woods are lovely, dark, and deep, and it comes as no surprise to the listener when the merchant picks a rose from the garden for Beauty and a beast rushes out and growls, "Your daughter or your life!" It's one of the oldest themes in literature: The beautiful young girl learns to love a beast, thereby breaking the spell and restoring him to human form.

Once upon a time an editor called and told me that one of the illustrators she worked with, Barry Moser, had long been fascinated by the story and wanted to illustrate it. Could I retell it for him?

I said no. Why retell what has been told beautifully in the first place? The editor pointed out that there is no single, correct version of "Beauty and the Beast." Many old versions exist, and she sent me some to look at. I read them with curiosity and admiration. They were different from one another yet true in the way that fairy tales have always been true: they hold up a mirror to our deepest wishes and fears.

Still I said no and explained to her that I was already hard at work on another story. A story? It felt more like a fish that kept slipping away from me. Every time I picked it up I found scenes that didn't belong for all sorts of reasons. Here was a scene I'd added because a friend had told me a funny anecdote and I wanted to include it for the same reasons that as a child I had once put olives into my ice cream: I loved olives and thought the ice cream could only be improved by so delicious an addition. Well, it wasn't. And here was an opening scene I'd written to give information I thought the reader should have as early as possible. The opening pages creaked under the weight of my reasons for writing it, which had nothing to do with the real story. Finding the real story is hearing the voice of the story itself and following it. Suddenly I thought how pleasant it would be to write a narrative in which I didn't have to discover the story. So I agreed to write yet another version of "Beauty and the Beast."

The Beast and his magic mansion in the forest—that's what most of us love about the tale, isn't it? We can hardly wait for Beauty to leave her father and sisters behind so that we can enter the kingdom of the Beast. But what does the Beast look like? The traditional storytellers say only that he was frightful. Sitting in my living room, I discussed this problem with the one person who had to know the answer: Barry Moser. Was the Beast an animal? A human, badly deformed? My one-eyed cat walked round and round us, eavesdropping, now and then pausing to give Barry an odd look.

When I started working with the original story, I felt as if I'd mounted a wise horse that knew exactly where to go and the best way of getting there. And why shouldn't it have known? It had been making the trip for years, and the road was as fresh as it was when, once upon a time, the first teller of that tale laid it down. Why not give the old story a new time and place? New York at the turn of the century. I had the plot, the characters, the time, the place. This would be smooth sailing. Very soon I discovered the error of my ways.

Here is the opening of a traditional version of "Beauty and the Beast":

> There was once a very rich merchant, who had three
> daughters; being a man of sense, he spared no cost for their
> education, but gave them all kinds of masters. His daughters
> were extremely handsome, especially the youngest; when
> she was little everybody admired her, and called her "the
> little Beauty" so that, as she grew up, she still went by the
> name of Beauty, which made her sisters very jealous. The
> two eldest had a great deal of pride, because they were

rich. . . . They went out every day upon parties of pleasure, balls, plays, concerts, etc. and laughed at their youngest sister, because she spent the greater part of her time in reading good books.

Trying to retell this was a humbling experience. That expensive education, for example. Did the daughters of the wealthy go to boarding school or did they have governesses? What and how were they taught? And those parties of pleasure mentioned so casually in the third sentence: What did it feel like to be a guest at one at the turn of the century in New York? And what does it feel like to be rich?

To find out, I turned to the biographies of people who had had firsthand knowledge: J. P. Morgan, Cornelius Vanderbilt, Andrew Carnegie, John Jacob Astor. I skimmed and scanned, looking for the singular detail or observation that would make my own story believable. And the more I read, the more I heard my own memories waking and muttering: Remember that party your cousin Sue took you to in Grosse Pointe when you were fifteen? Remember the receiving line, the young girls descending the staircase, the young men leaning in the doorways? Remember the white gloves you wore? You wondered what the other girls would say if they knew your daddy was not a stockbroker or an auto manufacturer but a college professor. You wondered what the young men would say if you told them you wanted to be a writer.

Four months after embarking on this project, I had enough courage to write the first paragraph of my *Beauty and the Beast*:

Long ago, when the century was still young, a rich merchant lived with his three daughters in a splendid town-house in New York. The house looked out on Central Park on Fifth Avenue at Fifty-ninth, and the merchant had filled the house with treasures from his travels, tapestries and candelabra, chests and cameos, marble angels and bronze beasts. In the evening, when lights blazed in every window, men in white waistcoats and women a-glitter with jewels were ushered into the dining room where a long dinner table covered with gold damask and gold china and the finest crystal awaited them. Behind every highbacked chair stood a footman. And beyond the French doors lay the greenhouses and gardens. The merchant favored orchids and roses.

The traditional stories do not say exactly where the merchant took his family after he lost his money, but I could not get off so easily. It seemed likely they would head north to one of the little towns along the Hudson. But which town? The countryside around Saugerties is different from the country around Highland, and the countryside around Rhinebeck is different from both of them. Nevertheless, I felt on sure ground, for I know something about small towns along the Hudson and something about living in the country and quite a lot about the business of keeping a garden, washing clothes, cleaning house, and cooking dinner.

But when I started to write this part of the story, I found out all over again how much you have to know in order to write a single line. What would Beauty see and hear and smell in the country at the turn of the century? Of course, there were no supermarkets, no refrigerators, no laptop computers, no message machines, no Federal Express, and no freeways. There were also no traffic jams, and no parking problems. Beauty would have traveled to the nearest town by horse, and she would have been able to recognize far more birds and wildflowers than I can. In winter, without central heating and insulation and down jackets, she would have felt the cold more keenly than most of us. Along the river she would have seen men chopping huge blocks of ice and carrying them away to underground storage rooms where the blocks would stay until they were called for in warm weather. Beauty would have kept the family provisions in a root cellar under the kitchen floor, hauled water from a well, washed in the creek, and cooked meals on a wood-burning stove. When Beauty sets off across the frozen fields to meet the Beast, she is leaving behind a life filled with passages of great sweetness and chapters of great hardship. Life in the magic mansion hidden along the Hudson is surely a glorious change, in spite of its ugly owner.

The magic mansion presented a new problem. What did it look like, feel like—both inside and out? This is the moment you can either throw up your hands or invoke that patron saint of writers, Saint Chance. Her creed is simple: What you need, you shall find. But you will never find her if you don't believe in her power to help you, the power of things beyond your control. One of her most devoted followers was James Joyce, who said: "Chance furnishes me what I need. I am like a man who stumbles along; my foot strikes something, I bend over and it is exactly what I want."[10] While García Márquez was writing *Love in the Time of Cholera,* he relied on Saint Chance as well. To an interviewer he confessed that at the end of the day, "when the sun started going down I would go out on the street to look for places where my characters would go, to talk to people and pick up language and atmosphere. So the next morning I would have fresh material I had brought from the streets."[11] When you are deeply immersed in writing your story, chance can become a magnetic field that draws you to the very people and places you need to finish it. Whatever passes through that field—conversations, books, movies, letters, dreams—seems to belong to the story itself.

What Saint Chance sent me was a mansion called Wilderstein, fifteen miles up the Hudson River from where I live. The ninety-seven-year-old woman who resided in it was born and raised there, the last surviving member of her clan. Like the merchant, her father had lost his money during a depression. Unlike the merchant, he did not lose his land. The moment I spied the house—dark, looming, with turrets and weathervanes rising over the surrounding trees—I said to myself, What a perfect mansion for the Beast! In the foyer there was a bronze dragon coiled around the newel post, which threw a sinuous shadow on the Tiffany windows over the landing. The andirons in the fireplace looked as if they might bark or howl at a stranger; they had the shape of griffins, with glass eyes that glowed when a fire was lit. There was gold damask wallpaper in the living room and a coat of arms in the dining-room window. Soon I found myself calling this mansion the Beast's house.

When I sat down to write the scene in which Beauty enters the Beast's house, Miss Gatherer whispered: "This will be easy. Since the Beast's house is a real place, you have only to take notes on it and describe it." I did exactly as Miss Gatherer instructed me, and the writing went badly. The scene was cluttered, the language dull. What started by inspiring me ended by fettering me. And finally I understood what Miss Experience was trying to tell me all along: The Beast's house in the story is magic, and magic has nothing to do with real estate. The gift of the mysterious mansion was not a real gift until I let it go. For a writer, knowing what to save is tricky business. Ben had taught me that years before, when I met him in the beer hall in Heidelberg. Trust your own imagination. Travel light. It takes very little baggage to get where you're going.

At Ben's burial service, how little he took with him: his grand-father's prayer book, placed on his coffin by his mother; and a handful of pink tulips tossed into the grave by those of us who would remember him till our own stories were ended. *Ubi sunt?* We turned to go back to the cars. It was a sunny day, a windy day in February. Ben's mother said, "I saw three crows by my window last week. I think they were an omen." A friend of Ben's whom I did not know touched my arm and said, "Will you put all this into a story?"

His question came, I think, not from curiosity but from the hope that somebody could gather up the pieces of Ben's death and make something new. Something that will last.

NOTES

[1] François Villon, "The Ballad of Dead Ladies," in *The Testaments of François Villon,* John Heron, trans. (New York: Boni and Liveright, 1924), 295.

[2] "Godfather Death," *The Complete Grimm's Fairy Tales* (New York: Pantheon, 1972), 211–12.

[3] John Stone, M.D., "Listening to the Patient," *Literary Cavalcade* 27 (Feb. 1990); reprinted from the *New York Times,* 1988.

[4] Robert Hendrickson, *The Literary Life and Other Curiosities* (New York: Viking, 1981), 28.

[5] Nancy Willard, "Clearing the Air," in *Carpenter of the Sun* (New York: Liveright/Norton, 1974), 6.

[6] Ezra Pound, "Dr. Williams' Position," *The Dial* 85 (Nov. 1928): 398.

[7] Robert Coles, M.D., *The Call of Stories* (Boston: Houghton Mifflin, 1989), 23.

[8] Marcel Proust, *Remembrance of Things Past, Vol. I: Swann's Way* and *Within a Budding Grove,* C. K. Scott Moncrieff and Terence Kilmartin, trans. (New York: Random House, 1981), 47–48, 50.

[9] Mary Weaver, "The Home of Healing," *Storytelling Magazine* (Summer 1989): 20.

[10] Brenda Maddox, "Joyce, Nora and the Word Known to All Men," *New York Times Book Review,* May 15, 1988: 1.

[11] M. Simons, "The Best Years of His Life: An Interview With Gabriel García Márquez," *New York Times Book Review,* April 10, 1988: 48.

Permissions Acknowledgments

"High Talk in the Starlit Wood; On Spirits and Stories" reprinted by permission of the *Michigan Quarterly Review*, Winter 1986, vol. xxv, no. 1.

"The Watcher" reprinted, with permission, from *Innocence and Experience: Essays and Conversations on Children's Literature* (1987, Lothrop); edited by Barbara Harrison and Gregory Maguire.

"Looking for Mr. Ames" reprinted by permission of the *Michigan Quarterly Review*, Summer 1989, vol. xxviii, no. 3.

"When by Now and Tree by Leaf" reprinted with permission of the Children's Literature Association.

"Newbery Acceptance Speech" by Nancy Willard, from *The Horn Book Magazine,* 1982.

"Telling Time": reprinted from *Prairie Schooner* by permission of the University of Nebraska Press. Copyright 1988 by the University of Nebraska Press.

"Close Encounters of the Story Kind" first appeared in the *New England Review.*

"Something That Will Last": reprinted from *Prairie Schooner* by permission of the University of Nebraska Press. Copyright 1991 by the University of Nebraska Press.

"Egg" reprinted from *PM/AM, New and Selected Poems,* by Linda Pastan, by permission of W. W. Norton & Company, Inc. Copyright © 1982 by Linda Pastan.

"The Wife of Usher's Well" from *The Viking Book of Folk Ballads* by Albert B. Friedman, editor. Copyright © 1956 by the Viking Press, Inc. Used by permission of Viking Penguin, a division of Penguin Books USA Inc.

"The Witch of Coos" from *The Poetry of Robert Frost* edited by Edward Connery Lathem. Copyright 1951 by Robert Frost. Copyright 1923, © 1969 by Henry Holt and Company, Inc. Reprinted by permission of Henry Holt and Company, Inc.

"John Kinsella's Lament for Mrs. Mary Moore" reprinted with permission of Macmillan Publishing Company from *The Poems of W. B. Yeats: A New Edition,* edited by Richard J. Finneran. Copyright 1940 by Georgie Yeats, renewed 1968 by Bertha Georgie Yeats, Michael Butler Yeats, and Anne Yeats.

"The Waking" copyright 1948 by Theodore Roethke, from *The Collected Poems of Theodore Roethke* by Theodore Roethke. Used by permission of Doubleday, a division of Bantam Doubleday Dell Publishing Group, Inc.